Keep Fit in Grammar

Grammatisches Übungsbuch
für die Klassen 9–13

von Peter Lampater, Peter Pasch
und Paul Aston
unter beratender Mitarbeit von
Rosemary Hellyer-Jones

Ernst Klett Verlag
Stuttgart München Düsseldorf Leipzig

Preface

Aims and target groups

Keep Fit in Grammar is a book of grammar exercises for intermediate students of English; the book can be used either as course material in class or for revision purposes.
The material covers all basic English grammar and concentrates especially on those areas that German learners tend to find difficult.
The contents of *Keep Fit in Grammar* are based on *Learning English – Grundgrammatik – Ausgabe für Gymnasien* (Klettbuch 51151) and its English equivalent *A guide to Grammar* (Klettbuch 51153), but the exercises can also be used with any other grammar or any other course materials.
The exercises are on the whole straightforward and lend themselves to quick and efficient revision of specific areas of English grammar. While the easier exercises might be satisfactorily dealt with even in the 3rd or 4th year of English, the more demanding ones can offer a challenge even to "Grund-" or "Leistungskurs" students.
At the back of the book there is a short list of grammatical structures that German students very often find particularly difficult to use correctly. This list is by no means comprehensive but simply highlights a few 'tricky points'.
Chapter and section headings are identical with those of the *Grundgrammatik* so that students and teachers can easily compare the exercises with the corresponding rules and examples. Apart from the references to the *Grundgrammatik* (GG 20 = Grundgrammatik § 20), there are also references to the *Grammatik des heutigen Englisch* (Klettbuch 5057) or its English equivalent *A Grammar of Present-Day English* (Klettbuch 5058) for a more in-depth analysis of structural phenomena. (GhE 57 = Grammatik des heutigen English 57).
The vocabulary used in the book is based on *Learning English – Green Line*, and any words that an intermediate student of English is not likely to be familiar with have been explained.

Types of exercises

The exercises vary in length, difficulty and complexity, with the first exercise(s) in each separate section normally being quite easy, while the exercises towards the end of chapters tend to be more demanding.
Each chapter also contains a number of translation exercises. These exercises present an efficient way of checking and revising differences between German and English usage.

How to use the book

Obviously, it is not necessary to work through the material in the order in which it appears. It may be advisible to start off with the section or sections in the *Grundgrammatik* that students are interested in or want to revise, reading the examples and the rules carefully. Then the corresponding exercise(s) could be done and the answers checked with the teacher or the *Key* (Klettbuch 50622). And then, in order to uderstand what went wrong, the *Grundgrammatik* should be consulted again.

Contents

Note:
[ ] In translation exercises, German words in square brackets are not to be translated.

Chapter 1: Nouns

The singular and plural forms of nouns GG 2; GhE 69–70

1 *What are the plural forms of these nouns?*

1. address 2. aircraft 3. bath 4. beach 5. belief 6. biro 7. cargo 8. child 9. deer 10. dictionary 11. enemy 12. fish 13. fly 14. foot 15. goose 16. handkerchief 17. hero 18. hoof 19. knife 20. life 21. loaf 22. mouse 23. nobleman 24. ox 25. piano 26. potato 27. roof 28. scarf 29. sheep 30. tooth 31. video 32. wife 33. woman

Now put the plural forms in the correct groups, according to their ending:

a) . . .s: *baths, . . .*
b) . . .es: *addresses, . . .*
c) . . .ies
d) . . .ves
e) singular = plural
f) irregular forms

2 *What do you call these? Use compound nouns.* (GG 2.1A; GhE 71)

1. Husbands of daughters
2. People who walk past in the street
3. Children of the age of eight
4. Sisters of wives or husbands
5. People who are grown up
6. Mothers of wives or husbands
7. People who drive buses
8. Machines you use for washing dishes

Nouns used only in the singular GG 3; GhE 73.1 + 3, 76

3 *Translate into English:*

1. Kannst du mir ein paar Ratschläge geben?
2. Die Nachrichten gestern Abend waren wirklich schlecht.
3. Die Informationen, die sie uns gab, waren sehr hilfreich.
4. Unsere neuen Möbel sehen gut aus, nicht wahr?
5. Die Hausaufgaben waren leicht. Ich hatte sie in einer halben Stunde fertig.
6. Deine Haare sehen super aus. Wo lässt du sie schneiden?
7. Seit Ende des Zweiten Weltkrieges sind die USA das mächtigste Land der Welt.
8. Seine Kenntnisse über die Vereinigten Staaten sind wirklich beeindruckend.

4 *Which is the odd man out in each group? Can you say why? (Because it is the only noun in the group that is singular/plural, countable/uncountable, . . .)*

1. luggage – traffic – equipment – machine – furniture
2. politics – games – maths – althletics – physics
3. advice – fact – knowledge – progress – information
4. factory – engine – tool – machinery – robot
5. the Great Lakes – the United States – the West Indies – the Bahamas – the Rocky Mountains

5 *Put in* is *or* are:

1. Politics . . . taught at many universities.
2. . . . comics really worth reading?
3. . . . the Netherlands a member of the EC?
4. The news . . . on TV now.
5. The United States . . . the leading power in NATO.
6. Darts . . . played in most English pubs.
7. Statistics . . . often incorrect.
8. Physics . . . one of the few subjects I really enjoy.

Nouns used only in the plural
GG 4; GhE 73.2 + 4

6 *What do you call them? Choose from the words below*

binoculars, glasses, goods, people, the police, pyjamas, scissors, scales, stairs, surroundings, tights, wages

1. They are between floors and you walk up and down them.
2. You earn them – when you work.
3. They are always around you.
4. Lorries carry them to shops, which sell them.
5. Men, women and children.
6. You can see things in the distance with them.
7. You use them to weigh things.
8. They are like long stockings, and women wear them.
9. They are worn by people who can't see well.
10. You wear them in bed.
11. You cut with them.
12. You call them if you notice a crime.

7 *Translate into English:*

1. Wo ist meine Brille? Ich kann sie nirgends finden.
2. Sei vorsichtig auf der Treppe. Sie ist sehr steil.
3. Der Lohn für diese Arbeit ist zu niedrig.
4. Die Umgebung Londons ist sehr interessant.
5. Diese Schere ist nicht scharf genug. Ich kann mit ihr nicht schneiden.
6. Ist deine Hose neu? Sie sieht gut aus.
7. Die Polizei ist da. Hast du sie gerufen?
8. Die Waage ist in der Küche. Du findest sie im Schrank.

Expressions of quantity
GG 5; GhE 73.2, 114

8 *Look at David's holiday list. What is he taking? What is he leaving at home? Use the correct expressions of quantity.*

luggage	1	jeans	2
books	2	shorts	1
maps	1	pyjamas	1
sunglasses	0	pullovers	0
scissors	0		

He's taking one/two (piece(s)/pair(s) of . . .
He's not taking a pair of . . . /any . . .

9 *Sandy has been shopping. What has she bought? Use the correct expressions of quantity. (Do not use "some".)*

She has bought
a/one . . .
two . . .
three . . .

10 *What are the English words for these German expressions? Put them in the blanks. Don't forget to add the correct expression of quantity.*

Brillen, Brot, Gepäck,
ein Glas Wasser, Information,
eine interessante Nachricht,
einen Rat, Scheiben Brot

1. Have you got . . .? – Yes, but only a small bag and this rucksack here.
2. What would you like to drink? – Just . . ., please.
3. How many . . . shall I cut? – Perhaps ten or twelve. – We've only got one . . . left, though.
4. You know Scotland so well. Couldn't you give me . . . on where to stay in Edinburgh?
5. I've just heard . . . on the radio.
6. I need two . . ., one for reading and one for watching TV.
7. That really is an interesting . . . . Have you told anyone else?

11 *Put the parts together to form sensible sentences and choose the correct form of the verbs:*

1. Half of the time in class
2. Half of my friends
3. A great number of birds
4. The majority of teenagers
5. The rest of the money
6. The rest of the visitors
7. Ten pounds
8. 5 kilometres
9. Six months

(has/have) just left.
(flies/fly) to Africa in winter.
(is/are) more than I can afford.
(is/are) wasted.
(is/are) too long to wait.
(is/are) a long way to walk.
(was/were) spent on sweets.
(is/are) away today.
(plays/play) video games.

s-genitive and *of*-phrase

GG 7; GhE 90–94

12 *Write out these sentences, choosing the correct form of the words given in phonetic transcription:*

1. My ['peərənts] are away on holiday.
2. My ['peərənts] bedroom is upstairs.
3. The ['tʃɪldrənz 'kəʊts] are in the wardrobe.
4. Is this your [ɑ:nts] umbrella?
5. The United Nations stands for peace among the ['pi:plz] of the world.
6. What will be the ['pi:plz] decision in the referendum next Sunday?
7. Mrs Copper is an ethnologist. She's been to many African countries to study the ['pi:plz] religions and customs.

13 *Which 's is a genitive, and which is a verb? Which can be both?*

1. Dad's gone
2. Dad's socks
3. My friend's younger brother
4. Kate's back
5. Today's the day
6. The dog's got a collar on
7. Kate's book
8. The dog's collar
9. My friend's younger
10. Today's paper

14 *Make sensible sentences, using either an* s-*genitive or an* of-*phrase:*

1. (the Millers/house) is at (street/end).
The Millers' house is at the end of the street.
2. Who is (this novel/author)? – Well, look at (page 13/top).
3. The (children/bikes) are at (garage/back).
4. What was (place/name) again? Perhaps it's in (yesterday/paper).
5. Our (neighbours/cat) always makes a mess in our garden. And then he sits on (wall/top) and grins.
6. My (brother/birthday) is at (June/end).
7. (Charles/friends) are all together at (bus/ front).

Chapter 2: Articles, demonstrative pronouns and determiners

The definite article
GG 9; GhE 105–106, 137A

1 *Put in* the *if necessary:*

1. ... houses in this town are not as expensive as ... houses usually are. 2. ... house we bought cost £180,000. 3. ... estate agent who sold it to us was called Johnson. 4. ... estate agents like him get 1.5% when they sell a house, and as ... people nearly always sell ... houses through ... estate agents, they are ... ones who have ... money to buy ... biggest houses. 5. A lot of ... people like ... houses with ... big gardens. 6. I prefer ... small gardens. 7. ... houses in the centre of the town are ... ones that have ... gardens I like – they're small, with ... walls round them.

2 *Use* the *if necessary:*

1. The concert is		next Tuesday.
2. My favourite month is		June.
3. School begins on		first Monday in September.
4. What would you like for		breakfast?
5. I'll never forget	(the)	August we went to France.
6. We're going to Scotland at		Christmas.
7. Do you remember		Christmas we had all that snow?
8. Did you enjoy		dinner you got on the plane?

3 *Fill in the gaps using one of the nouns above the sentences, together with the definite article if necessary:*

1. **school – bike – bus**
   I usually go to ... by ..., but when it rains I take .... leaves at 8.40 and arrives at ... at 8.50. ... starts at 9, so I have to hurry.
2. **church – Sunday – car**
   Our family usually goes to ... on .... We usually go by .... We can park ... in the car park outside ....
3. **hospital – life**
   My aunt wanted to visit a friend in ... yesterday. On the way to ... she had an accident and had to be taken to ... herself. – ... can be strange. My grandfather nearly died when he tried to save ... of his neighbours' cat.
4. **train – work – dinner**
   John Hastings goes to ... by ... every ... day. He always takes ... to do on ..., but today ... is so crowded that he can't concentrate. He intends to do some of ... at home after ... instead.

4 *Translate the following sentences into English:*

1. Ich gehe hin und wieder in die Kirche; aber oft ist die Kirche fast leer.
2. Wir trafen uns jeden Tag nach der Schule.
3. Das größte Gebäude in unserem kleinem Dorf ist die Schule.
4. Wo gingen Sie zur Schule?
5. Ich war schlecht in der Schule.
6. Frau Brown wartet gerade auf den Bus. Sie fährt immer mit dem Bus in die Stadt.
7. Er muß ins Krankenhaus.
8. Betty arbeitet im Krankenhaus.
9. Was hatten Sie zum Mittagessen?
10. Nach dem Mittagessen ging sie zum Arzt.
11. Das Mittagessen, das wir im Hilton Hotel aßen, war hervorragend.
12. Er verbrachte die meiste Zeit im Schwimmbad.

13. Spielen Sie ein Instrument? – Ja, ich spiele Klavier.

5 *Put in* the *if necessary:*

1. ... history is full of ... wars and ... disasters.
2. ... music was her life.
3. ... life is full of surprises.
4. I never thought much about ... death, until ... death of my grandmother.
5. I have got an interesting book about ... history of England.
6. Many people say that ... women have more imagination than ... men.
7. ... love is like ... war: easy to begin, but hard to end.
8. I hate ... women because they always know where ... things are. (James Thurber)

6 *Translate the following sentences into English:*

1. Die meisten Leute in Deutschland verstehen Englisch.
2. Die meisten Schüler mögen keine Grammatik.
3. Die intelligentesten Menschen sind nicht immer [auch] die erfolgreichsten.
4. Die meisten von ihnen konnten überhaupt kein Deutsch verstehen.

The definite article with names
GG 10; GhE 107

7 *Translate the following sentences into English:*

1. Gestern abend hat der alte Tom seinen Enkeln ein schönes Märchen erzählt.
2. Bensons haben kein Auto.
3. Der Snowdon ist der höchste Berg in Wales, der Mont Blanc der höchste in Europa.
4. Die zwölfjährige Linda Scott hat den ersten Preis gewonnen.
5. Kennst du Sandersons?
6. Der Central Park in New York ist größer als der Hyde Park in London.
7. Der Tower und der Buckingham Palast werden jedes Jahr von vielen Touristen besucht.

8 *Make sentences using these words:*

1. MontBlanc/Alps/south/France
   Mont Blanc is in the Alps, in the south of France.
2. Ludgate Hill/City/London
3. Isle of Man/Irish Sea
4. Appalachians/eastern side/United States
5. Rhine/most important river/Western Europe
6. St Lawrence River/flows/from/Lake Ontario/to/Atlantic
7. Falkland Islands/near/Argentina
8. Loch Ness/west/Scotland
9. Oxford Street/main street/City/Westminster

9 *Put in* the *if necessary:*

1. ... most people like swimming, especially outside in ... sun in ... July or in ... August. 2. But there is a group of people in England who swim outside all ... year, even in ... winter. 3. They are in ... Serpentine Swimmers Club. 4. ... most people don't even want to take off their coats or scarves when ... temperature is minus five degrees. 5. But these people take off all their clothes, put on their swimming things and swim in ... lake in ... Hyde Park in London. 6. Sometimes they have to break ... ice before they can go into ... water! 7. Every Christmas Day these people all swim in ... lake together. It doesn't matter if it's absolutely freezing. 8. To make things worse, they swim very early in ... morning!

The indefinite article
GG 11; GhE 103.1

10 *Translate the following sentences into English:*

1. Mr Hall ist Bäcker.
2. Ralph ist Protestant, aber seine Freundin ist Katholikin.

3. Susan möchte Schauspielerin werden.
4. Antonio ist Italiener und Gunnar ist Schwede.
5. Kennedy war von 1961–63 Präsident der Vereinigten Staaten.
6. Im Jahre 1990 wurde Mr Nelson Bürgermeister unserer Stadt.
7. Ken hat Kopfschmerzen.
8. Unser Direktor ist immer in Eile.

11 *Complete the texts, adding* a *or* an *where necessary:*

Elizabeth I became . . . in	queen
1558 when her sister	
Mary died. Their father	
was Henry VIII, who was	
. . . until 1547. His father	king
was Henry VII, who was	
. . ., but was not even . . .	Welshman –
when he was born. Mary	prince
was . . ., but Elizabeth was	Catholic
. . .. Mary's husband was	Protestant
. . ., Philip of Spain, who	Spaniard
like his wife was . . .	Catholic

Anne Smith became . . .	manager
of the local supermarket	
in 1995, when her boss	
left to become . . . in	manager
York. Until then, Anne	
had worked as . . . in the	assistant
office. Anne's father is	
. . . of the local news-	editor
paper and . . . of the	president
town sports club. Her	
mother is . . . from Toron-	Canadian
to. She met Anne's father	
when she first came to	
England as . . .. Today	student
she is	British citizen

The indefinite article with units of quantity and time GG 12; GhE 103.2

12 *Translate into English:*

1. Die Kartoffeln kosten 60 p das Pfund.
2. Die Post wird nur einmal am Tag abgeholt.
3. Auf dieser Straße dürfen Lastwagen nicht schneller als 80 km pro Stunde fahren.
4. Stadtführungen finden nur zweimal in der Woche statt.
5. Die Kekse kosten ein Pfund pro Packung.

The position of the definite and the indefinite article
GG 13; GhE 102, 104

13 *Translate into English:*

1. Der Flughafen ist eine halbe Meile entfernt.
2. Wir verbrachten die halbe Nacht auf dem Bahnhof.
3. Er hat den ganzen Kaffee getrunken.
4. Beide Jungen spielen hervorragend Fußball.
5. Was für eine gute Idee!
6. Es ist eine ziemliche Überraschung, dich hier in London zu treffen.
7. Wir haben noch nie einen so trockenen Sommer gehabt.
8. Sie war so in Eile, dass sie uns nicht bemerkte.
9. Im Mai hatten wir 10000 Besucher. Nächsten Monat erwarten wir die doppelte Anzahl.
10. Dies ist eine viel zu schwierige Aufgabe *(job)*.

Demonstrative pronouns and demonstrative determiners
GG 14; GhE 108–109

14 *Complete the sentences using* this, that, these *or* those:

1. I haven't had time to go to the library . . . week.
2. . . . is the new disco over there.
3. I'll take . . . two books here.

4. How much are ... CD players over there?
5. We saw "Crocodile Dundee" in 1990. ... was the last time I went to the cinema.
6. ... days, people don't read as many books as before there was TV. In ... days, people visited each other much more often, too.
7. Last winter, we had a lot more parties than we've had ... winter.
8. I've got an appointment with the manager at 10 o'clock ... morning.
9. Here's a photo of my two sisters: ... is Margaret and ... is Catherine.
10. ... biscuits are much better than ....

Chapter 3: Personal pronouns and determiners

Personal pronouns – The use of subject and object forms
GG 16; GhE 83

1 *Fill in the correct forms of the personal pronouns:*

1. Who's that? – ...'s ..., Jennifer.
2. Barbara said ... would be here by five. That must be ... now.
3. Jim and I would like to have a look at the photos. Could ... show ... to ...?
4. John is as tall as ..., but Peter is quite a bit taller than ... am.
5. When I saw Joan at the airport, I knew at once it was ....
6. Sue is a fantastic tennis player, but I'm better than ... at swimming.
7. Look, here comes Bonzo. Let's give ... a dog biscuit.
8. There was an awful cat miaowing in our garden last night. ... kept ... awake almost all night.
9. Our neighbours have got a much larger garden than ..., so ... get more fruit than ... do.
10. I keep forgetting to give that CD back to Susan. ... must remember to give ... to ... when ... next see ....

It, he, she* or *they* for German *es
GhE 84

2 *Translate these sentences into English:*

1. Es war sehr nett von dir mich einzuladen.
2. Wer hat angerufen? – Es war Carols Freund.
3. Es sind mindestens 20 Kilometer bis zur Grenze.
4. Wessen Auto steht vor der Garage? – Es ist Peters.
5. Es war mir nicht möglich, ihn zu erkennen.
6. Wer sind die beiden Jungen? – Es sind meine Cousins.
7. Kennst du einen Herrn Abernathy? – Ja, es ist unser neuer Englischlehrer.
8. Wer ist die alte Dame dort drüben? – Es ist meine Großmutter.
9. Wem gehören die Tennisbälle hier? – Es sind Anns.
10. Wer ist das an der Tür? – Es muss der Postbote sein.

General personal pronouns (*one, you,* etc.) GG 17; GhE

3 *Translate these sentences, using* you, one, they *or* people. *(Don't use the passive.)*

1. Man darf nicht alles glauben, was man im Fernsehen sieht.
2. Man sollte nie zu früh aufgeben.
3. Man sagt, dass San Francisco die schönste Stadt in den Vereinigten Staaten sei.
4. Man weiß nie, was passieren kann.
5. Im 15. Jahrhundert glaubte man, dass die Erde eine Scheibe sei. *(to be flat)*
6. Was wird dort drüben gebaut?
7. Von hier aus hat man eine gute Aussicht auf die Stadt.
8. In diesem Restaurant kann man wirklich gut essen.
9. Vergesst eure Schirme nicht. Man kann nie wissen.

Possessive determiners GG 18; GhE 96, 97

4 *Fill in the missing words:*

1. Tessa isn't at school this morning. ... has hurt ... arm, and so ... mother's taken ... to the family doctor.
   – Where's the doctor's surgery?
   – In Salisbury. Tessa's got all ... school things with ..., so if the doctor says ...'s all right, ... mother's going to take ... to school.
2. Put ... hat on, Mary – ...'s cold outside, and ... should cover ... ears. ...'ll need ... warm jacket, too. And gloves, to keep ... hands warm.
   – Oh, don't make such a fuss. Even if ... ears and fingers go red in the cold, ... won't die.
3. Did you enjoy ... holidays at ... aunt and uncle's?
   – Yes, we had a great time. The only thing that got on ... nerves was that they treated ... like small children. ... aunt always asked if ... had washed ... hands and faces and if ... had brushed ... teeth. And ... uncle told ... not to read in bed because ... thought ... was bad for ... eyes.
4. Children needn't have ... eyes tested every year. But the dentist should check ... teeth. Parents shouldn't forget to check ... children's shoes, too – children can easily damage ... feet if ... don't wear the right size.

5 *Translate these sentences into English:*

1. Warum ziehst du nicht den Mantel aus, wenn dir so warm ist?
2. Er hat immer die Hände in den Hosentaschen.
3. Sie schüttelte den Kopf und ging weiter.
4. Wenn ich die Augen schließe, kann ich besser hören.
5. Der Wind war sehr kalt, und wir setzten die Mützen auf.
6. Als die Einbrecher von der Polizei überrascht wurden, warfen sie die Pistolen weg und hoben die Hände hoch.
7. Er stürzte vom Fahrrad und brach sich das Bein.
8. Vor dem Essen müssen wir uns die Hände waschen.
9. Im letzten Jahr kamen zwei Schweizer Bergsteiger im schottischen Hochland fast ums Leben.
10. Sie haben jetzt ihre Meinung über die Gefahren dieser Berge geändert.

Possessive determiners + *own* GG 19; GhE 98

6 *Translate into English, using* one's own *or* of one's own:

1. Wenn wir umziehen, habe ich endlich ein eigenes Zimmer.
2. Hat deine Tante keine eigenen Kinder?
3. Wir haben das Haus nur gemietet, es gehört uns nicht.
4. Ich brauche dein Fahrrad nicht, ich kann mein eigenes nehmen.

5. Aber Tom hat kein eigenes Rad. Vielleicht kannst du ihm deins leihen.
6. Meine Großmutter lebt allein. Sie kocht selbst. Und geht selbst einkaufen. *(do one's cooking/shopping)*
7. Ihr könnt kommen, aber ihr müsst euer Essen selbst mitbringen.

Possessive pronouns GG 20; GhE 99

7 *Fill in the correct possessive pronouns. Decide whether to use* of.

1. This isn't my pen. Is it . . ., Clare?
2. Yesterday I met a cousin . . . in the High Street.
3. Our car broke down yesterday. So our neighbours lent us . . ..
4. Can I borrow your pocket calculator? I've forgotten to bring . . ..
5. The Simpsons asked me to call on a friend . . . who lives in York.
6. This looks like one of Susan's T-shirts. – Yes, it's one . . ..
7. While Peter and Jenny were in Birmingham, they stayed with an aunt . . ..
8. This can't be Timmy's anorak. . . . is blue, not green.
9. We aren't so keen on your CDs. I think those . . . are much better.

Pronouns ending in *-self/-selves* and reciprocal pronouns GG 21–22; GhE 86–88

8 *Finish these sentences, using pronouns ending in* -self/-selves*:*

1. Did you have your house painted? – No, we . . .
2. Can you please clean the windows in my room, Mum. – I'm sorry, but I'm busy at the moment; you . . .
3. Does someone look after your grandfather's garden? – No, he . . .
4. Do the Masons have their car washed every week? – No, they . . .
5. Does her aunt do the cooking for Gill while her parents are away? – No, she . . .
6. Did you have your hair cut? – No, I . . .
7. Will you write that letter for us, Dad. – Well, I expect you . . .

9 *Translate the sentences into English:*

1. Er stellte sich vor und sagte, sein Name sei Henry Miller.
2. Ich kann mich nicht daran erinnern, wo er wohnt.
3. Die Stadt hat sich sehr verändert.
4. Hat sich etwas Besonderes ereignet, während ich weg war?
5. Wir fragen uns, ob wir uns auf ihn verlassen können.
6. Setzt euch und entspannt euch.
7. Ich kann mir vorstellen, dass ihr müde seid.
8. Freust du dich auf die Reise?
9. Viele Kinder fürchten sich im Dunkeln.
10. Das Messer ist sehr scharf. Schneid dich nicht.
11. Seid ruhig und bewegt euch nicht.
12. Die Tür öffnete sich und ein Mann kam heraus.
13. Es ist spät. Wir müssen uns beeilen.
14. Wir haben uns gestern sehr schlecht benommen, wir sollten uns entschuldigen.

10 *Finish the sentences. Use* each other *or pronouns ending in* -self/-selves.

1. Sue looked at Tom and Tom looked at Sue. They . . .
2. She loves him and he loves her. They . . .
3. Joan enjoyed herself at the party and so did Gill. They . . .
4. The Joneses are very selfish. They never think of other people. They only . . .
5. Please don't pay for us. We can easily . . .
6. The policeman didn't see the burglar, and the burglar didn't see the policeman. They . . .
7. If you help me with the washing up, I'll help you with your homework. So we . . .

8. The Smiths have stopped buying Christmas presents. She doesn't give him anything, and he doesn't give her anything. They . . .

11 *Fill in a personal pronoun, a pronoun ending in* -self/-selves *or a reciprocal pronoun* (each other/one another):

1. Hey, John, can . . . come over for a moment? . . .'d like to introduce . . . to my friend from Dublin. – We know . . . already. . . . were introduced to . . . at Mary's party.
2. . . . have cream all over your faces. Just look at . . . in the mirror.
3. When Eddie and Brenda suddenly met on the stairs, . . . looked at . . . in surprise.
4. You look bored. Aren't . . . enjoying . . .? – Oh, yes, I'm enjoying . . . very much. . . . was just listening to that song.
5. What have you said to . . .? She seems hurt. – Nothing. . . . just feels sorry for . . . because nobody is paying attention to . . ..
6. Where's Tom? I haven't seen . . . yet. – . . .'s in hospital. . . . hurt . . . badly when . . . was cutting the grass.
7. Is there anything left to eat? . . .'m terribly hungry. – Yes, over there. Go and help . . .. Oh, could . . . bring . . . a sandwich, too?
8. Shall I help . . . to clean up? – No, don't worry. . . .'re all right. Tina and Mike are going to help . . ..
9. Can Linda and Chris stay here overnight? Their parents are away over the weekend and . . . have locked . . . out.

Chapter 4: Indefinite pronouns and determines

Some and *any* used as expressions of quantity GG 23; GhE 110–115

1 *Put in* some *or* any:

1. I haven't had . . . breakfast this morning. I'm getting hungry.
2. She had . . . biscuits and . . . cake afterwards.
3. Are there . . . interesting new shows on at the moment?
4. Let's buy . . . sausages for our party tonight.
5. Have you bought . . . new magazines recently?
6. We need . . . oil for the salad.
7. I'm afraid I didn't get . . . tomatoes today.
8. Can I have . . . crisps, please? – Certainly, here you are.
9. Have you got . . . writing pads? – Yes, what size would you like?
10. Would you like . . . more tea? – Yes, please.
11. Is there . . . sugar left? – No, I'm afraid there isn't . . ..
12. Hurrah, we haven't got . . . homework today!
13. Steve never takes . . . books with him when he goes on holiday.
14. Oh dear, there is hardly . . . tea left.

2 *Translate these sentences into English using* some *or* any:

1. Brauchen wir Zucker? – Nein, wir brauchen keinen Zucker, aber wir brauchen Tee.
2. Ich habe gestern keine Birnen gekauft.
3. Ich habe heute sehr schöne Äpfel – 30 p das Pfund.
4. Haben sie Tomatenketchup?
5. Er bot mir etwas Schokolade und etwas Tee an.

Some, any, no and their compounds
GG 24–25; GhE 115, 120–121

3 *Put in the missing indefinite pronouns or determiners*:

1. Carol? There's ... on the phone for you.
2. What would you like to drink? – ..., thanks. I'm not thirsty.
3. Could... help me to set the table, please?
4. There's ... cake left. Did you eat it? – I only ate a small slice. ... else must have eaten the rest.
5. Let's make ... special for dinner today. How about a chicken curry with rice?
6. How many tomatoes are there left? – ... at all. I used them for the salad.
7. Has ... seen the bread knife? I must have left it ... near the telephone, but I can't find it ....
8. ... wanted to try ... of the hamburgers because they smelled so terrible.
9. ... of the shops I tried had ... tomatoes.
10. That stew tastes delicious. Where did you find the recipe? – .... I invented it myself.

Much and *many*
GG 26; GhE 116–117

4 *Fill in* much, many *or* a lot of. *Use* much *or* many *wherever possible.*

1. We always have ... homework to do.
2. We don't have ... free time.
3. Are there ... boys in your class?
4. This essay took me ... effort.
5. How ... pages have you written?
6. I can't come to the swimming-pool today, I've got too ... to do.
7. I haven't done ... sport this year.
8. Do you play ... matches against other schools?
9. You've made so ... mistakes in this text that it's hard to understand.

5 *Fill in* much, too much, too many *or* a lot (of):

It's time for a change. This government has made far ... mistakes and spent ... time doing nothing. ... people are now asking how ... longer we have to wait for a new government. We have to pay far ... tax in this country – that's because there are far ... people spending our money. They should get their hands out of our pockets – is that ... to ask? ... the time, we don't know where the money goes. The government thinks we don't care ..., but we do. We care ....

6 *Replace* (a) little *or* (a) few *by equivalent expressions*:

Examples:

There is **little** money left.	=	There is **not much/hardly any** money left.
There is **a little** money left.	=	There is **some/a bit of** money left.
He has **few** friends.	=	He does**n't** have **many** friends./He has **hardly any** friends.
He has **a few** friends	=	He has **some/a small number of** friends.

1. Unfortunately, only a few people survived the earthquake.
2. After his tour through Europe he had little money left.
3. During our language course in England we had little time left to enjoy ourselves.
4. Normally one sees few tourists in our part of Scotland.
5. If you have a little time, look at a few churches in the city.
6. There are a few Chinese restaurants in this part of the town.
7. Ireland has little industry.
8. Very few people want to spend money on bad films.

Every, each, any, all (the) and the compounds of *every* and *any*
GG 28–29; GhE 124–125

7 *Decide which of the forms in brackets to use:*

1. I get up at 8 o'clock (all/every) day.
2. Let's go on. We can't stay here (all/every) day.
3. They sell (all/all the) kinds of things at the market.
4. Fresh water freezes at a higher temperature than salt water, but (every/all/each) water freezes when it gets really cold.
5. (All/Each) of the children has a skateboard.
6. (All/Each) of us play table-tennis.
7. (All/All the) shops in town are closed today.
8. Who has eaten (all/all the) chocolate?
9. Not (all/all the) chocolate is brown.
10. There's a bus to the city centre (all/each/every) twenty minutes.

8 *Fill in* every *(or a compound) or* any *(or a compound)*:

1. Do you meet him often? – Yes, he comes to see us . . . Friday he is in town.
2. Are you ready? – Yes, we can leave . . . time.
3. Shall I sit here, or here? – It doesn't matter. You can sit . . . you like.
4. . . . in the village knows where we live. If you can't find our house, ask . . . in the street.
5. Is . . . all right? – Yes, . . . is fine.
6. What would you like to drink, coffee, tea, orange juice? – Oh, . . ., as long as it is non-alcoholic.
7. It's easy to put up that tent. . . . child could do it.
8. My uncle is too lazy to walk. He goes . . . by car, even to the newsagent's round the corner.

Both, either, neither
GG 30; GhE 122–123

9 *Translate into English, using* both, (the) two, either *or* neither:

1. Die beiden Jungen sahen sich an. Beide waren überrascht.
2. Ich habe beide nicht gesehen.
3. Alle beide wollten in den Zoo gehen.
4. Ich wollte euch allen beiden danken.
5. Seine beiden Brüder mögen Tierfilme.
6. Er ist über beide verärgert.
7. Keiner meiner Brüder spielt Fußball, aber sie interessieren sich beide dafür.
8. Ich kann den Ball mit jeder Hand fangen.
9. Ich kenne keinen der beiden.

Chapter 5: Numbers and expressions of time and place

Enumerations and expressions of frequency GG 31, 33; GhE 161, 358

1 *Fill the gaps using* firstly, secondly, *etc. or* once, twice, *etc.*:

"Are you sure you don't want to come to the cinema tonight?"
"Yes, quite sure, for several reasons: . . ., I have already seen the film . . . on TV, and I'm not keen on seeing it a third time. . . ., I want to go to bed early tonight, and . . . I don't like going to the cinema, anyway. I haven't been to the cinema even . . . this year."
"Don't you ever go out in the evening?"
"Oh, yes, I go to the youth club . . . or . . . a week: every Tuesday and Thursday, and sometimes on Fridays, too."

Prepositions in expressions of time GG 35, 59; GhE 171–173

2 *Translate the following sentences:*

1. Es war 3 Uhr morgens.
2. Er fährt an Weihnachten in Urlaub.
3. Am Sonntagmorgen gibt es bei uns Rührei zum Frühstück.
4. Morgens habe ich nie Hunger.
5. Am Morgen des 6. Juni 1944 begann der D-Day.
6. Sie trafen sich an einem schönen Samstagmorgen.
7. Am letzten Donnerstag traf ich meinen Freund in London.
8. Sie kommt am nächsten Montag.
9. An meinem Geburtstag gebe ich eine große Party.

3 *Fill in the gaps using one of the following words:*

after, ago, at, before, between, by, for, from, in, on, since, till/until, to

(Sometimes there is more than one correct answer.)

Sue is an actress. She joined the *Princess Theatre* three years . . ., and she has been playing leading roles . . . over a year.
Sue never goes to bed . . . 2 am, and she usually gets up . . . 10 and 11. . . . some days, when she has gone to bed much later than two the night . . ., she even sleeps . . . 11 or longer. . . . one o'clock she goes out for lunch with her boyfriend. Later . . . the afternoon, she does some shopping or goes for a walk, but she is usually back home . . . four.
She has to be at the theatre . . . five for rehearsal *(Probe)*. Rehearsal is . . . five . . . six, or . . . six . . . eight . . . days when there is no performance . . . the evening.
Tonight there is a performance . . . 7.30 . . . 9.45. The play has been running . . . January this year. . . . the performance, Sue is going to a party. It will probably last . . . 3 o'clock . . . the morning, but Sue wants to be home . . . two, because she has to learn a new part for tomorrow.

4 *Fill in either* since *or* for:

1. He has been living in London . . . 1980.
2. She has been wearing glasses . . . she was three.
3. I haven't seen him . . . last week.
4. I haven't seen him . . . two weeks.
5. This book has sold over a million copies . . . it was published.
6. It's a long time . . . lunch.
7. Until I met him last night I hadn't seen him . . . a long time.
8. After the accident she was unable to speak . . . several days.

Prepositions in expressions of place and direction   GG 36; GhE 164–170

5 *Look at the picture and fill in a suitable preposion.(Sometimes there is more than one correct answer.)*

1. Where is the plane? – It is . . . the sky.
2. Where are the boats? – They are . . . the lake.
3. Where is the boy with the balloon? – He is sitting . . . the tree.
4. Where is the tiger? – It is . . . the picture the girl is painting.
5. Where is the flag? – It is . . . the tent.
6. What is the old man doing? – He is leaning . . . the tree.
7. Where is the table? – It is . . . the chairs.
8. What are the seagulls doing? – They are flying . . . the lake.
9. What is the dog doing? – It is running . . . the lake.
10. Where are the four boys and girls? – They are sitting . . . the fire.
11. And the cats? – They are lying . . . each other.
12. Can you see any other animals? – Well, there are some sheep . . . the hills.

6 *Decide which of the two words to use:*

1. *among – between*

a) He put a cigar . . . his lips.
b) I found a photo of my great grandmother . . . the things in the attic.
c) . . . her luggage was a small cage with a dog inside.

2. *with – at*

a) We get our bread . . . the baker's in the High Street.
b) He has been living . . . his uncle since 1983.
c) He stayed . . . her until midnight.
d) He has been living . . . his aunt's for the last few weeks.

3. *towards – against*

a) She saw the child running . . . her.
b) The policeman leaned . . . his car.
c) The children were pressing their noses . . . the shop window.

4. *after – behind*

a) The policeman ran . . . the burglar, but wasn't able to catch him.
b) The sun disappeared . . . a cloud.
c) The boys stood . . . a tree.

5. *till/until – up to*

a) They didn't get back . . . 2 o'clock.
b) Read . . . page 77, please.
c) Wait . . . I come back.
d) There is room for . . . eight people in the minibus.

7 *How can you get from Hamburg to the centre of Manchester? Fill in suitable prepositions where necessary:*

You can catch a boat . . . Hamburg . . . Harwich . . . 16.30 . . . every second day. . . . Harwich, you get . . . a train . . . Piccadilly Station, the main station . . . Manchester. The train leaves Harwich . . . the arrival of the boat and reaches Manchester . . . five hours, so you are usually . . . Manchester . . . about 18.00 . . . the next day. On Sundays, you have to change . . . Birmingham New Street.

Or you can get . . . a plane . . . Hamburg . . . Manchester . . . every day. Planes leave Hamburg twice a day, . . . the afternoon, . . . 13.55, and . . . the evening, . . . 18.30. The airport is south . . . Manchester. You go . . . customs . . . the Arrival Hall. To get . . . there . . . the city centre, you walk . . . a long corridor and get . . . a train which takes you . . . Manchester Piccadilly.
. . . Piccadilly, you go . . . a bookshop, . . . a door and . . . some steps leading . . . a very busy street. Then you only have to walk . . . the road: there is a tram stop . . . the other side. The tram takes you . . . the city centre.

Chapter 6: The adjective

The formation of adjectives
GG Appendix 3.2; GhE 351.2

1 *Form adjectives ending in* -ous, -ious *or* -uous *from the following nouns:*

1. ambition
2. curiosity
3. danger
4. enormity
5. rebellion
6. fury
7. glory
8. nerve
9. fable
10. strain

2 *Add* -able *or* -ible *to the following:*

1. comfort-
2. improb-
3. incred-
4. notice-
5. poss-
6. sens-
7. suit-
8. terr-
9. unbeliev-
10. unbeat-

3 *Form adjectives ending in* -ive *from the following verbs:*

1. act
2. attract
3. create
4. decide
5. imagine
6. extend
7. represent

4 *Form adjectives ending in* -ic *or* -ical *from the following nouns:*

1. alcohol
2. alphabet
3. biology
4. fantasy
5. idiot
6. medicine
7. politics
8. publicity
9. type

Attributive and predicative use of adjectives
GG 37; GhE 131–133

5 *Use these adjectives to complete the sentences:*

ill – sick; asleep – sleeping; alive – living; afraid – frightened; alone – lonely

1. People living . . . often look upon TV as a friend.
2. Is Mike still . . .? – No, he woke up a few minutes ago.
3. After ten days without food the cat was still . . . but very weak.

4. . . . animals often eat grass.
5. The . . . mouse tried to escape into its hole.
6. . . . babies look like little angels.
7. Isn't Steve better yet? He's been . . . for over a week now.
8. Don't be . . . of the dog. He's quite harmless.
9. Now that my cousin has died, I have no . . . relatives left.
10. There are still some . . . country roads where driving can be fun.

6 *Translate these sentences into German:*

1. The train was late.
2. Henry was sick all over the floor.
3. We're having a late spring this year.
4. Four people in the class are reported sick.
5. The late king was not very popular.
6. I'm sick of it.

7 *Translate these sentences into English:*

1. Er ist der einzige Junge in der Klasse.
2. Ich bin froh, wenn ich manchmal allein sein kann.
3. Er stellte sich schlafend. *(pretend to)*
4. Schlafende Kinder sollte man nicht stören.
5. Hab keine Angst – der Hund bellt nur, aber er beißt nicht.
6. Ich bin oft schon um sechs Uhr wach.
7. Wer ist nach deiner Meinung der größte lebende englische Schriftsteller?
8. Ihm ist auf der Fähre schlecht geworden.
9. Ein glücklicher Mensch kann allein sein, ohne sich einsam zu fühlen.
10. Die Polizei fand die zwei verängstigten Kinder in dem alten Schloss.
11. Als meine Großeltern noch lebten, haben wir sie oft am Sonntag besucht.

Adjectives after certain verbs

GG 38; GhE 55, 56

8 *Make 9* ***sensible*** *sentences from this table:*

1.	The situation	was becoming	
2.	His teachers	were getting	bankrupt last week.
3.	The noise of the radio	grew	taller and taller.
4.	Visitors are asked	to keep	nice enough.
5.	With all that rain the grass	was growing	awake until well past midnight.
6.	When we first met Simon he	seemed	more and more dangerous.
7.	Last night I couldn't fall asleep.		louder all the time.
	I must	have stayed	quiet in the church.
8.	In spite of the danger she	remained	fed up with Tom's behaviour.
9.	I'm afraid Gerald has lost		calm.
	his job. His company	went	

9 *Complete the sentences with suitable adjectives or adverbs. Choose from the list of adjectives. (Sometimes there are several possibilities.)*

awful, careful, tired, good, happy, hungry, nasty, serious

1. One of the King's servants had to taste all the food . . . before serving it.
2. Although he eats such a lot he always looks . . ..
3. With that . . . cold her voice sounded . . . on the phone.
4. The cat looked . . . at the birds.
5. I'm . . . sorry, but there's something that smells . . . in this cupboard.
6. After the long bike ride they all felt . . ..
7. I'm afraid your son doesn't take his work . . . enough.
8. Timmy was . . . with his new computer. He tried it out . . ..
9. The plan sounds . . ., but we must look at it all again . . ., if everything is to go . . ..

Comparisons
GG 39–40, 47; GhE 136–139, 145–146

10 *Complete the table with the adjectives below:*

basic form	comparative	superlative
ambitious	. . .	. . .
. . .	more awkward	. . .
. . .	. . .	worst
. . .	. . .	. . .

ambitious, awkward, bad, beautiful, boring, careless, central, clever, cruel, dangerous, dry, expensive, famous, far, free, good, heavy, incredible, interesting, narrow, nervous, simple, thin, typical, wide

11 *Fill in a suitable form of the words in brackets (basic form, comparative or superlative). Sometimes there are several possibilities.*

1. The *(good)* day of that holiday was when we found a *(good)* place to go swimming than we had found the week before. The sea was *(warm)* than at that other place, the rocks were *(interesting)* than there and they were much *(far)* from the crowds, who used the much *(ordinary)* beach *(near)* the town. Our beach was right *(near)* the lifeboat house, and it was the *(far)* from the part which was *(dangerous)* for swimming.
2. "The *(unusual)* musical of the year!" said the poster. "The first visit of one of the *(famous)* musical companies in Europe." Unfortunately, the tickets were the *(expensive)* in Europe that evening, too – even the *(cheap)* seats were $ 40, and they were the *(terrible)* seats I have ever sat on. And the view was even *(bad)*. I couldn't see the singers at all. But the music was the *(bad)* thing about the whole evening. It was *(noisy)* than anything I had ever heard before, apparently played by the *(hopeless)* musicians in Europe.

12 *Make comparisons, using* (not) as . . . as *or* . . . than*:*

1. Chinese > English (difficult/easy)
   Chinese is more difficult than English./English is not as difficult as Chinese. English is easier than Chinese.
2. Jaguars > Volkswagens (expensive/ cheap)
3. Cheese < chocolate (taste good/bad)
4. Travelling by train > travelling by bus (quick/slow)
5. Glass > plastic (heavy/light)
6. Sydney in June < in January (hot/cool)
7. The body temperature of most birds > the body temperature of humans (high/low)
8. People on land > in the water (fast/slow)
9. The sun > the other stars (near/far away)

13 *Fill in* as *or* than:

1. A football is eight times ... heavy ... a tennis ball.
2. My car is far slower ... Tom's. It was far less expensive ... his, of course.
3. The exam results are not ... good ... I expected them to be.
4. Their team didn't play ... well ... ours.
5. The population of Germany is far larger ... the population of Britain.
6. This book seems more interesting ... that one, although it is far cheaper ... the other one.
7. There are about twice ... many people in New York ... there are in Los Angeles, but Los Angeles covers a far larger area ... New York.
8. English food used to be much worse ... it is today. Nowadays you can eat ... well in London ... you can in Paris.

14 *Fill in* than *or* then:

1. I'm bigger ... you, but ... I'm older ... you, of course.
2. It's my birthday next week – ... I'll be two years older ... you.
3. I'd rather have big feet ... big ears.
4. The festival was better ... ever this year.
5. What's all this about, ...?
6. I got up, cleaned my teeth and ... had breakfast.

15 *Rewrite the sentences as "rules of correlation", using* the + *comparative* ... the + *comparative* ...:

1. When the sea is calm, it is easy to swim. *The calmer the sea (is), the easier it is to swim.*
2. When roads are narrow, speeds have to be low.
3. When rules are simple, they are easy to understand.
4. When the weather is hot, pupils get sleepy.
5. When castles are very old, their walls are thick.
6. When the packaging looks attractive, the product is expensive.
7. When lessons are interesting, the pupils learn well.
8. When you work hard, you will do well.

The use of prop words and adjectives used as nouns
GG 41, 42; GhE 127–128, 134–135

16 *Decide whether to fill in* one *or* ones *or nothing. (Sometimes there are two possibilities.)*

1. Those apples look nice. Could I have two of these big ..., please?
2. Funnily enough you've got all the difficult questions right, but you've made a lot of mistakes in the easy ....
3. I'm afraid this fork is dirty. Could you get me a clean ...?
4. Are those your books? – No, those ... over there are mine.
5. What did you think of the film? – It was the best ... I've ever seen.
6. The Millers have three boys. The eldest ... is 24. He is the ... that lives in Australia.
7. Is that bike new? I always thought you had a black .... – It's not my own .... It's Sarah's ....
8. Fortune favours the brave .... *(Dem Mutigen gehört die Welt).*

17 *Translate these sentences into English:*

1. Die Reichen sollten die Armen unterstützen.
2. Die Jugendlichen halfen dem Blinden über die Straße.
3. Das Neue ist der Feind des Alten.
4. Viele Alte finden sich in der Welt von heute nicht zurecht. *(can't cope)*
5. Wo ist der Neue? Der Chef möchte ihn sprechen. *(to see s.o.)*
6. Die Kleine spielte mit zwei Katzen, einer weißen und einer schwarzen.
7. Heute wird mehr für die Behinderten getan als vor 100 Jahren.

8. Vor dem Bürgerkrieg lebten nur wenige Schwarze in den Nordstaaten der U.S.A.
9. Hast du „Die Nackten und die Toten“ gelesen?
10. Das Komische an der Geschichte ist, daß die Tote am Ende wieder lebendig wird. *(to come to life)*
11. Das Beste an dem Plan ist, dass die Jungen und die Alten zusammenkommen können.
12. Ein Gesunder findet es oft schwierig, sich die Probleme von Kranken vorzustellen.

Adjectives and nouns expressing nationality GG 43; GhE 361

18 *Complete the table:*

She is from	She is a(n)	She prefers . . . food/music/ etc.	She speaks	She thinks the . . . are the nicest people in the world.
1. Australia	. . .	. . .	. . .!	. . .
2. . . .	. . .	Austrian	. . .!	. . .
3. . . .	. . .	. . .	. . .!	Bavarians
4. Belgium	. . .	. . .	. . .!	. . .
5. . . .	. . .	. . .	. . .!	Canadians
6. . . .	Chinese	. . .	. . .	. . .
7. Denmark	. . .	. . .	. . .	. . .
8. . . .	. . .	French	. . .	. . .
9. . . .	German	. . .	. . .	. . .
10. . . .	. . .	. . .	Dutch	. . .
11. . . .	. . .	. . .	. . .!	Irish
12. . . .	. . .	. . .	Italian	. . .
13. . . .	. . .	. . .	. . .!	Mexicans
14. . . .	. . .	. . .	Japanese	. . .
15. Poland	. . .	. . .	. . .	. . .
16. . . .	. . .	Portuguese	. . .	. . .
17. Russia	. . .	. . .	. . .	. . .
18. Scotland	. . .	. . .	. . .!	. . .
19. . . .	. . .	. . .	. . .	Spanish
20. . . .	. . .	. . .	. . .!	Swiss
21. . . .	. . .	. . .	Turkish	. . .
22. the U.S.A.	. . .	. . .	. . .!	. . .

Chapter 7: Adverbs and adverbial phrases

Adverbs and adjectives

GG 38, 44–45; GhE 56, 140, 143

1 *Adverb or adjective? Put in the right form of the words in brackets:*

1. Some people think that motor racing is . . . stupid. (real)
2. She was . . . unable to answer the question. (total)
3. I was . . . shocked to hear about your . . . accident. (deep / terrible)
4. This computer programme is . . . . You can . . . work with it. (easy)
5. My friend can speak English . . ., and she also speaks . . . French. (fluent / excellent)
6. Does your sister drive . . .? – Yes, she is a . . . driver. (good)
7. This child needs medical attention . . . . (fast)
8. Susan is . . . . . ., and she is always . . . dressed. (remarkable / pretty / good)
9. Their flight did not take . . ., but they had a . . . journey to the airport. (long)
10. The helicopter pilot had to fly . . . because the clouds were very . . . . (low)
11. A . . . newspaper is a paper which is delivered . . . . (daily)
12. Today's cricket match ended . . . because of bad light. (early)
13. In the . . . chapters of the novel Agatha Christie describes a "perfect" murder. (early)
14. The taxi driver was really . . . . He spoke to me . . . . (friendly)
15. Deborah has had a . . . operation. She is . . . ill. (serious)
16. After the match she felt . . . . (exhausted)
17. Don't eat your food so . . .! TIt's such a pity, especially when the meal tastes so . . . . (quick/ delicious)
18. It all sounded so . . . that I began to laugh. (crazy)
19. Van Gogh's work was not taken . . . until . . . after his death. (serious / long)
20. This fish looks . . ., but it smells . . . . (fresh / awful)
21. The dog looked . . . at the postman. (angry)

2 *Choose one of these adjectives for each of the sentences and decide which form to put in – adjective or adverb:*

angry, awful, bad, careful, fast, perfect, quiet

1. It's a small car, but it is very . . . around corners. You can drive it surprisingly . . . .
2. He was very . . . . He shouted at his son . . . .
3. I'm . . . tired. I've had an . . . day.
4. Martin speaks . . . Spanish. He really speaks Spanish . . . .
5. Our teacher told us to be . . . . However, we didn't stop talking, but went on speaking more . . . .
6. It really was a . . . earthquake. Our house was . . . damaged.
7. My wife always drives . . ., especially at night. She's always been a . . . driver.

3 *Translate the following sentences into English:*

1. Der Hund da drüben sieht gefährlich aus.
2. Fühlen Sie sich vor Aufführungen nervös?
3. Warum schaust du immer so ernst drein?
4. Er sah mich ernst an.
5. Die Besucher sahen sich neugierig um.
6. Der Kellner probierte den Wein kritisch und sagte, er schmecke gut.
7. Diese Milch riecht schlecht.
8. Der Stoff fühlt sich weich und warm an.

Adverbs: Double forms with different meanings GG 46; GhE 144

4 *Complete the following sentences by using a suitable adverb:*

just/justly,	pretty/prettily,	fair/fairly,
late/lately,	hard/hardly,	high/highly

1. I realized my mistake too . . ..
2. Don't you think you have been spending too much time on your hobbies . . ..
3. She turned up . . . as we were leaving.
4. The police think that they acted . . ..
5. After her holiday in Spain she had . . . any money left.
6. They tried . . . not to laugh.
7. We go skiing . . . often.
8. If you don't want to play . . ., let's stop the game altogether.
9. The guests praised the food . . ..
10. The castle stands . . . upon the hill.
11. When she saw the photographers, she smiled . . ..
12. I'm . . . sure I'm right about that.

5 *Translate the following sentences into English:*

1. Er hat heute kaum etwas gegessen.
2. Herr Watt hat sein ganzes Leben hart gearbeitet.
3. Ich habe die Flasche gerade geöffnet.
4. Mein Vater war zu Recht ärgerlich.
5. Mein Bruder spricht ziemlich gut Spanisch.
6. Er ist ein guter Spieler, aber er spielt nicht immer fair.
7. Ich bin ziemlich sicher, dass sie sich auf meiner Party amüsieren werden.
8. Schau mal, wie hübsch sie ihr Klassenzimmer dekoriert haben.
9. Ich hatte gestern [noch] spät am Abend ein Telephonat.
10. Meine Mutter war in letzter Zeit nicht gesund.
11. Sieh mal, wie hoch dieser Ballon fliegt.
12. Sie ist hochqualifiziert.

Adverbs in comparisons GG 47; GhE 145–146

6 *Fill in the missing forms of the adverbs:*

basic form	comparative	superlative
quietly	more quietly	most quietly
. . .	. . .	most carefully
well	. . .	. . .
. . .	more	. . .
often	. . .	. . .
. . .	more easily	. . .
. . .	. . .	most interestingly
fast	. . .	. . .
. . .	. . .	worst
little	. . .	. . .
. . .	more regularly	. . .
hard	. . .	. . .
straight	. . .	. . .
early	. . .	. . .
. . .	. . .	most truly
slowly	. . .	. . .
soon	. . .	. . .

7 *Complete the following comparisons:*

1. He didn't want to disturb us. So he came in . . . possible. (quietly)
2. After seeing the accident he drove . . . than before. (slowly)
3. She speaks much . . . than he does. (clearly)
4. The small dog was barking . . . than the big one. (noisily)
5. In the mixed doubles Bob played much . . . than his sister. (badly)
6. After your phone call I got here . . . I could. (quickly)
7. Let's play tennis together . . .. (often)
8. We nearly had an accident there. Please drive . . .. (carefully)

8 *Make comparisons as in examples a)–c):*

a) drive fast – Tom = Peter
Tom drives as fast as Peter.

b) read a lot – Kate < Jack
Kate doesn't read as much as Jack./ Kate reads less than Jack./Jack reads more than Kate.

c) work hard – Paul < Susan < Kevin
Paul works hard. Susan works harder. Kevin works hardest.

1. speak English well – Jill = Kate
2. paint badly – Jack = Kevin
3. work hard – Tina < Susan
4. play tennis well – Liz < Mike
5. enjoy swimming (much) – Paul < Simon
6. read little – Tina < Paul < Simon
7. enjoy cooking very much – Sarah < Sally < Toby
8. play chess badly – Tom < Jenny < Jack

9 *Fill in either* good, well, better *or* best:

1. He did very ... in the test, ... than expected.
2. Your homework was not really ...; I think you can do much ....
3. Guy doesn't speak ... English; a year ago he spoke ... than he does now.
4. I quite like swimming, although I like football ...; but I really like cycling ... of all.

10 *Translate the following sentences into English:*

1. Bitte sprechen Sie lauter und deutlicher.
2. Kate singt genauso schön wie ihre Mutter.
3. Tom macht seine Hausaufgaben sorgfältiger als seine Schwester.
4. In Japan fahren viele Züge schneller als in Europa.
5. Peter rannte, so schnell er konnte.
6. Du solltest öfter in die Kirche gehen.
7. Jill kleidet sich modebewusster *(fashionable)* als ihre Klassenkameradinnen.
8. Er kam früher an als erwartet.

Types and position of adverbs
GG 48–53; GhE 141–142, 147–155

11 *Put the adverbs in the position you think best:*

1. John sings. (well)
2. Sally passed her driving test. (easily)
3. She speaks German. (fluently)
4. His friends left. (suddenly)
5. Please close the door. (quietly)
6. At first the two children played together, but later they quarrelled. (happily/violently)
7. My father got up and left the room. (furiously/immediately)
8. The bus stopped. (noisily)
9. They could see the reasons for his decision. (clearly)
10. Black clouds began to cover the sky. (slowly)

12 *Add one of these adverbs to each of the sentences. (In most cases, there are several possibilities.)*

awfully, extremely, far, greatly, much, pretty, quite, really, very

1. Do you love me?
2. I'm fed up with these endless meetings.
3. I agree with you.
4. Are you sure this is the right address?
5. I'm sorry for being late.
6. It was nice of you to have come.
7. She was too polite to criticize him.
8. He speaks French better than German.
9. I prefer cooking to washing up.
10. We admired our new music teacher.

13 *Put the words in the right order to make sensible sentences. (Sometimes there are several possibilities.)*

1. never well-kept looks the park
2. bottles full of is usually the dustbin
3. washes a cleaner the floor sometimes
4. my father an egg always has for breakfast
5. soon got the children with their toys bored
6. a pond have always we in the garden had
7. never the road built been have should
8. Denis have soon finished will his exams
9. have never here we moved should
10. the door lock always when go out you

14 *Translate into English:*

1. Ich habe das Buch nur einmal gelesen.
2. Er hat gestern seinen Freund besucht.
3. Nächste Woche ist er nicht mehr da.
4. Die Blumen müssen jeden Tag gegossen werden. *(water)*
5. Er hat vor zwei Tagen seinen Geldbeutel verloren.
6. Susan hat schon viermal in Wimbledon gespielt.
7. Letzte Woche waren wir im Schwarzwald.
8. Er muss jeden Monat zum Arzt gehen.
9. Ich habe den Film 1994 gesehen.

15 *Connect these sentences using adverbs of comment:*

1. We arrived before the rain started. That was fortunate.
   Fortunately, we arrived before the rain started.
2. They will be there. I'm certain of that.
3. It was surprising. The old man could lift quite heavy things.
4. Her mother saw us just then. That was unfortunate.
5. She was very disappointed. We could understand that.
6. There should be snow on the ground at Christmas time. That would be ideal.
7. They did not have much experience. That was quite obvious.
8. One thing was clear: they had made up their minds.
9. They may have buried the money in the garden. That is quite possible.
10. We were lucky. We had wonderful sunshine all day.

The order of different adverbials in a sentence GG 54–55; GhE 160

16 *Answer the questions, using full sentences and the words given in brackets:*

1. How did they come over to England? (by car)
   They came over to England by car.
2. How long have you been living in this town? (for a year)
3. Where did you go for your holidays in 1994 (to Switzerland)
4. What did you do after school yesterday? (went swimming)
5. When did you leave the house this morning? (at 8 o'clock)
6. When does the film start on Saturday? (at 5.15)
7. What do you do on Sundays? (play hockey at sports ground)
8. How did you travel to London last week? (by plane)

17 *Complete the sentences by putting in the adverbs and adverbial phrases in their correct order:*

1. They came . . . | last Saturday/here |
   They came here last Saturday.
2. We drove . . .
   | for the weekend/to Liverpool |
3. He went . . . | to his room/quietly |
4. She went . . . | early/to bed |
5. They acted the play . . .
   | yesterday/at the church/exceptionally well |
6. The coach leaves . . .
   | on Friday/at 5 a.m. |
7. We're travelling . . .
   | by train/to Rome/next week |

8. The two men jumped ...

| to the ground/quickly |

9. Shakespeare hasn't been performed ...

| at our theatre/since I was a girl/so well |

18 *Combine the sentences below into single sentences:*

1. A dog barked outside the door. It barked loudly.
   A dog barked loudly outside the door.
2. We went to the museum. We went in a taxi. We went the following afternoon.
3. The teams are going to the playing fields. They are going on Saturday. They are going in the school minibus.
4. Jamie opened the door last night. He opened it with a spoon.
5. "The Bill" is shown on Fridays. It is shown at 8 pm. It is shown on TV.
6. She reads her post every morning. She reads it in the kitchen. She reads it before breakfast.
7. The crowd rushed out at the end of the match. They rushed out in panic.

19 *Translate into English:*

1. Letztes Jahr fuhren wir für ein paar Tage nach Edinburgh.
2. Mein Freund hat gestern den ganzen Tag lang in seinem Büro gearbeitet.
3. Deine Uhr ist wahrscheinlich im Schwimmbad gestohlen worden.
4. Letzten Montag bin ich mit dem Taxi zur Schule gefahren.
5. Er spielt oft mit seinen Freunden Fußball.
6. Susan spricht ganz gut Deutsch.
7. Unglücklicherweise war das Wetter in Italien die ganze Zeit schlecht.
8. Wir fahren oft übers Wochenende nach Cornwall.

Chapter 8: The tenses of the verb

The use of the simple and progressive forms: basic principles

GG 56; GhE 181–185

1 *Answer these questions. Use the words in brackets.*

1. What are you doing at the moment? – (I – learn – English grammar)
2. Where does Carol live? – (She – live – San Francisco)
3. What was Peter doing when you rang up? – (He – work – his computer)
4. When did you get home last night? – (I – get home – 10 o'clock)
5. How long has Wayne been learning German? – (He – learn – three years)
6. How does Jenny get to work? – (She – go – by bus)
7. What does Mr Black do? – (He – work – as a computer analyst)
8. Who is Mark talking to? – (He – talk – his girlfriend – on the phone)

2 *Complete the questions:*

1. When ... your father ...? – He retired when we was 65.
2. What book ...? – I'm reading a science fiction novel.
3. What ... yesterday? – We played tennis in the afternoon and then had supper.
4. What ... when Tom appeared? – We were having lunch.
5. She's an excellent skier. – How long ...? – She's been skiing since she was five.
6. Susan is an old friend of mine. – How long ...? – We've known each other for ten years.

7. What ... David ...? – He's a sales representative.
8. Who ... this car ... to? – It belongs to the manager.
9. We were watching the news when the TV broke down. – What time ... down? – At quarter past seven.
10. Where ... from? – I'm from Leeds and my friend is from Hull.

3 *Translate these sentences into English:*

1. Ich überlege, ob ich aufgeben soll.
2. Du bist heute wirklich sehr unfreundlich.
3. Ich glaube, sie kommen aus Dublin.
4. Sie trank *(have)* gerade eine Tasse Kaffee, als er sie anrief.
5. Nach dem Essen werde ich immer müde.
6. Hast du bemerkt, dass er eine neue Jacke anhat?
7. Ich weiß nicht, wie lange wir Gerald schon kennen.
8. Das Haus gehört den McAlisters schon seit Generationen.
9. Laß uns aufhören, ich werde müde.
10. Wen schaust du an? – Sarah. Sie sieht gut aus, nicht wahr?

The present tense: simple and progressive forms

GG 57; GhE 186–188

4 *Put in the simple or the progressive form of the present tense:*

1. The sun ... in the west, not in the east.	set
2. Money ... on trees.	not grow
3. More people ... Chinese than English.	speak
4. Lots of pupils ... to school by bus.	go
5. We often ... sandwiches for supper.	have
6. Sometimes our neighbours ... their car in front of our garage.	park
7. In "Little Red Riding Hood" the little girl ... a cake to her grandmother, who ... in the midst of a large forest. On her way she ... a wolf who ... to her and ... her where she	take, live, meet, speak, ask, go
8. I ... sorry. I ... busy at the moment. I ... the washing-up.	be, be, do
9. Look, the sun ... behind those hills.	go down
10. This book I ... is about a professor who ... with one of her students and ... to realize that he ... someone else.	read, fall in love, no want, love
11. It usually ... a lot here in August, but today it	not rain, pour

5 *Translate these sentences into English:*

1. a) Gill duscht jeden Morgen.
   b) Sie kann nicht ans Telephon kommen, sie duscht gerade.
2. a) Simon macht seine Hausaufgaben immer im Bus.
   b) Guck, da sitzt er. Er macht wieder seine Hausaufgaben.
3. a) Oliver frühstückt noch, er kommt aber gleich.
   b) Er isst *(have)* immer drei Scheiben Toast zum Frühstück.
4. a) Mary arbeitet für eine amerikanische Firma.
   b) Im Moment arbeitet sie an einem Projekt in Las Vegas.
5. a) Er trägt gewöhnlich Jeans.
   b) Heute trägt es seinen besten Anzug.
6. a) Er geht mir auf die Nerven. Dauernd erzählt er mir von seinen Erfolgen.
   b) Aber er erzählt mir nie von seinen Misserfolgen.

The present perfect: simple and progressive forms
GG 58–59; GhE 191–193

6 *Add suitable sentences using the present perfect and words in brackets:*

1. I'm afraid Robin won't be able to play on Saturday. . . . (break leg)
   He's broken his leg.
2. How come you're walking everywhere? – . . . (sell car)
3. There isn't any orange juice left in the fridge. . . . (we – drink)
4. Sandra's hair looks lovely. . . . (be – hairdresser's)
5. I'm not hungry. . . . (just – have breakfast)
6. My bike has disappeared. . . . (someone – steal)
7. Would you like a cup of tea? . . . (just – make)
8. I can't find Philip anywhere. – . . . (just – leave)
9. I've been looking for my keys all over the place. But I can't find them. I'm afraid . . . (lose)
10. Have you got any stamps? . . . (write letter to Grandma)

7 *Ask the questions. Use the words in brackets.*

1. . . .? – No, it hasn't. (the wind – drop – yet)
2. . . .? – She's been at sea since Tuesday. (how long – Cora – be)
3. . . .? – He's gone down to the cabin. (where – your father – go)
4. . . .? – No, she hasn't finished it yet. (Joanna – finish her sailing course)
5. . . .? – Yes, they went there last year. (parents – ever – be – Boat Show)
6. . . .? – They've stayed there three or four times. (how often – the Hayletts – stay – Harbour Hotel)
7. . . .? – No, I've never seen it. (see – ever – the film "Jaws")
8. . . .? – He's always wanted one. (how long – your dad – want a boat)

8 *Answer these questions using full sentences with the words in brackets. Decide whether to use* for *or* since *in your answers.*

1. How long has Carol been learning Spanish? (four years)
2. How long has it been raining now? (this morning)
3. How long have you been living in Aberdeen? (1985)
4. How long have you had a beard? (ages)
5. How long have Alan and Barbara been married? (last summer)
6. How long has Chris been watching TV? (came home from school)
7. How long have you been skiing? (I was five)
8. How long has that house belonged to the family? (the last century)

9 *Translate these sentences into English:*

1. Ich kenne Clare seit Weihnachten.
2. Das ist Herr Benson. Er ist seit September hier an der Schule.
3. Das Schloss gehört der Familie seit dem Bürgerkrieg.
4. Er fühlt sich den ganzen Tag schon schlecht.
5. Sie hat das Motorrad seit ihrem 18. Geburtstag.
6. Deine dreckigen Socken liegen nun schon seit Tagen unter deinem Bett.
7. Sie lieben sich seitdem sie sich zum ersten Mal im Kindergarten begegneten.
8. Wir warten nun schon seit über einer halben Stunde auf den Bus.
9. Ich habe jetzt genug. Seit heute Morgen arbeite ich nun schon im Garten.
10. Ihr spielt jetzt schon seit drei Uhr. Seid ihr noch nicht müde?
11. Hoffentlich kommst du aus der Garage raus. Es hat die ganze Nacht geschneit.

The past tense: simple and progressive forms

GG 60; GhE 189–190

10 *Complete the sentences using the simple past of these verbs:*

be, beat, bite, break, buy, catch, choose, come, cost, forget, go, hit, put, run, see, send, shoot take, wear, write

1. The Duchess ... to Harrods on Friday and ... some new clothes.
2. John ... Oliver 7 : 6, 6 : 3 in the first round.
3. When she ... near the dog it ... her.
4. Robin Hood ... an arrow, and it ... the Sheriff.
5. I ... lots of photos when I ... in France.
6. We only ... them a Christmas card last year, but they ... us a long letter.
7. When the boys ... the policemen they ... away.
8. Yesterday I ... the keys in my jacket pocket, but then I ... a different jacket and ... about them.
9. The Eskimo ... the ice and ... a fish.
10. She ... the most expensive of the three rings. It ... a fortune.

11 *Complete the jokes. Choose from the list of verbs, using the simple past.*

answer, ask, be, buy, not come, fall, find, happen, have, hit, lay, move, need, say, take, want

1. Until the year 1983, I never ... an accident. Then I ... a car.
2. Woman in restaurant: "What's the matter with these eggs?"
   Waiter: "Don't ask me, madam. I only ... the table."
3. "So your uncle ... down the stairs?" – "Yes, but he ... to come down anyway."
4. "How ... the accident ... ?" – "The sign ... STOP, LOOK, LISTEN – and while I was doing so, the train ... me."
5. "How ... you ... the steak sir?" – "I ... a pea and guess what? There it ...."
6. Pickles: "I'm worried about my brother. He's been thinking for years that he's a hen."
   Doctor: "Good gracious. Why ... you ... to me before about this?"
   Pickles: "Well, we ... the eggs."
7. The other day my dad ... the dog to the vet.
   The vet ...: "What's your dog's name?"
   My dad ...: "I don't know. He won't tell us."

12 *Complete the questions. Use the simple past. The words in brackets will help you.*

1. ... do last night?	We went to the theatre.
2. ... play ... see?	Julius Caesar.
3. ... performance ... ? (start)	At 7.30.
4. ... before the play? (do)	We had a meal.
5. ... the interval ... ? (last)	From 8.45 to 9.
6. ... during the interval? (go)	Onto the balcony.
7. ... the play ...? (finish)	At 10.20.
8. ... seats ...? (have)	Dress circle seats.
9. ... tickets ...? (cost)	Twenty pounds.
10. ... the play? (enjoy)	Yes, very much.

13 *Complete the sentences with the simple past or the past progressive of the given verbs:*

1. They ... about pollution	still argue
when we	leave
2. We ... tea outside in the	have
garden when it suddenly ... to rain.	begin

3. What . . . you . . . when I . . . last night? – I . . . a book.	do ring read
4. It . . . hard when the car . . . into the tree.	snow run
5. When he . . . the news, he . . . to laugh.	hear start
6. It . . . rather late, so they all . . . home.	get go
7. When we last . . . them, they . . . up that mountain path.	see climb
8. David . . . the car and . . . the key in his pocket.	lock put
9. Everybody . . . terribly busy. Peter . . . his bike, Louise . . . her homework, and Bonzo . . . his head off.	be repair do bark
10. When we . . . to the theatre, I . . . that I . . . the tickets with me.	get realize not have

Past tense and present perfect in contrast GG 61; GhE 194–195

14 *Fill in the correct form of the verb, past or present perfect (simple or progressive):*

1. The Joneses . . . to America last week.	fly
2. When we . . . to Heathrow we . . . the Underground to Paddington Station.	get take
3. How often . . . you . . . to London?	be
4. They . . . anything from her since she . . . to live in Montreal three years ago.	not hear go
5. We . . . for a bus for ages, but we . . . one yet.	wait see
6. . . . you . . . any pictures when you . . . Sea World?	take visit
7. Have another piece of cake. – No, thank you. I . . . three.	already have
8. Aunt Margaret . . . to New York in 1985. She . . . there for over 10 years now. But she . . . up on the Empire State Building yet.	move live not be

15 *Ask questions with the words given in brackets:*

1. That pullover looks great. (Where/buy?)
2. You seem to be rather tired this morning. (When/go to bed last night?)
3. You **are** friendly to Martin. (How long/know?)
4. I can't find Miss Hardcastle anywhere. (go home already?)
5. I took a taxi after the party last night. (How/**you**/get home?)
6. Peter is upstairs, doing his homework. – (How long/work?)
7. David is still in hospital. – (When/have the accident?)
8. Surely you can't be hungry already. (What time/have breakfast this morning?)

16 *Answer these questions, using* ago, for *or* since *with the expressions in brackets.*

1. How long have you had that car? – (Christmas)
2. When did the Scotts move to Detroit? – (three years)
3. How long has it been snowing? – (six hours)
4. What time did you have breakfast? – (two hours)
5. How long has Sam been living in Paris? – (1988)
6. When did you get the last letter from him? – (five months)
7. How long has she had that nasty cold? – (Saturday)
8. What time did you finish your homework? – (half an hour)

17 *Translate into English:*

1. Letztes Jahr haben wir die Ferien zu Hause verbracht.

2. Wann hast du ihn zuletzt gesehen?
3. Wir sind um halb fünf hier angekommen. Und nun warten wir schon über eine Stunde auf unseren Zug.
4. Waren Sie schon einmal in Australien?
5. Heute morgen bin ich erst um 8 Uhr aufgewacht.
6. Wir aßen gerade zu Mittag, als der Postbote klingelte.
7. Wo hast du diese tolle Bluse gekauft?
8. Als John anrief, habe ich mir gerade die Haare gewaschen.
9. 1992 sind wir das letzte Mal zusammen Skifahren gegangen.
10. Seitdem sie nach Nottingham gezogen sind, haben wir nichts mehr von ihnen gehört.

The past perfect: simple and progressive forms GG 62; GhE 196–197

18 *Complete the sentences using the past tense or the past perfect (simple or progressive) of the verbs on the right:*

1. After we . . . in New York	be
for three days, we . . . on	go
to see the Niagara Falls.	
2. President Kennedy . . .	not be
President long, when	
he . . . in 1963.	be shot
3. At last the plane	arrive
We . . . at the airport for	wait
two hours.	
4. Before Kim . . . on holiday	go
to New Zealand, she . . .	read
lots of travel guides about	
the country.	
5. Colin . . . for the company	work
for only two or three years,	
when he . . . one of their	become
top executives.	
6. When we . . . to the theatre,	get
the performance	begin/ already
7. At last the fire engine . . .,	come
but the house	burn down
8. Judy . . . with Mike	go out
for over a year, when	
she suddenly . . . that	decide
she . . . to see him	not want
any more.	
9. When the police finally	
. . ., the burglars	arrive
. . ., of course.	run away
10. Joy . . . to go on the	not want
school excursion to	
Hampton Court because	
she . . . there several times	be
with her family before.	
11. We . . . for five hours	climb
when we at last . . . to	get
the top.	
12. When I . . . my wallet,	find
all the money	be stolen

19 *Connect these sentences, using the given verbs and conjunctions:*

1. The alarm clock . . .	wake
me at three in	
the morning.	
I . . . it wrong the	set/because
evening before.	
The alarm clock woke me at three in the morning because I had set it wrong the evening before.	
2. I . . . my car in the	not find
airport car park.	
I . . . which deck	forget/because
it was on.	
3. They . . . all very	be
hungry. They . . .	not have/because
anything to eat since	
breakfast.	
4. Paul . . . a window	break
with his football.	
He . . . not to play	be told/although
football in the garden.	
5. We . . . off.	set
We . . . everything	put/as soon as
in the car.	
6. Grandmother . . . her	take
pills. She . . . better.	feel/after

7. He . . . the newspaper away. He . . . it. — throw, read/after
8. We . . . him for ages. He . . . such a popular actor. — know, become/before
9. The waitress . . . to clear the table. We . . . eating. — start, finish/before

Ways of expressing future time
GG 63–69; GhE 198–206, 208–209

20 *Say what these people are going to do. These words will help you:*

buy ice-cream, do washing up, break into house, get petrol, get married, plant tree, fly

1. *The driver in picture one is going to get some petrol.*
2. . . .

21 *Say what you think is (not) going to happen in these situations. These expressions will help you:*

be blown into, be late, be seasick, fail/not pass, get sunburnt, miss plane, run into, stop/prevent from using, win easily

1. A girl is running towards an English school building. The clock on the school says 9.10.
   She's going to be late.
2. A car is coming down a hill. There's no one in it. There are some trees at the bottom of the hill.
   The car . . .
3. The score is 6 : 2, 5 : 1 to Jimmy.
   He . . .
4. Sandra hasn't worked for her exams. She doesn't know anything about the subject.
   She . . .

5. A man is walking along the pavement. He's reading a paper and isn't looking where he's going. There's a lamppost in his way.
   He . . .
6. Aunt Emily is on the ferry from Folkestone to Calais. There are enormous waves.
   She . . .
7. A woman near you falls asleep on the beach. The sun is very hot, and she's only wearing a bikini.
   She . . .
8. Two jolly young men are leaving a pub, walking unsteadily towards their car. A policeman is watching them from the distance.
   He . . .
9. You are in a café beside a swimming-pool. There's a very strong wind, and your neighbour has left her hat on the table beside the pool.
   The hat . . .
10. The traffic jam has delayed us by half an hour at least. And it's another 50 miles to the airport.
   We . . .

22 *Look at Wanda's desk diary and say what she is doing this week. Use the present progressive of the following verbs:*

bake, do, go hiking, go to (2×), have taken, have tested, make/prepare, meet, play, visit

25	Mon	*3 p.m. hospital (Aunt Dorothy)* *8 p.m. cinema (Mike)*
26	Tue	*maths test (3rd and 4th periods)*
27	Wed	*4.30 tennis (Barbara)*
28	Thurs	*4 p.m. Dr. Edwards (eye test)*
29	Fri	*afternoon: salad/cake for party* *8 p.m. party (Mike's place)*
30	Sat	*passport photo* *3 p.m. Anne (in town)*
31	Sun	*off to Dartmoor (Mike, Barbara, Dean)*

23 *Look at the arrangements for your school visit to London. Form questions using the words in brackets and the present progressive.*

9.00	Meet at airport (When?)
13.15	Mr White meets us in London (Who?)
13.30	Bus takes us to host families (How/get?)
15.00	Everyone meets in Lyall School to arrange programme for visit (Where?)
18.00	To host families for supper (Where/have supper?)
19.00	Disco (What/do?)
21.00	Speech by Rolf to thank hosts (When/make?)
22.00–23.00	Our band plays (How long?)

24 *React to these questions and statements, using the expressions in brackets and the* will-*future:*

1. How old is your grandmother? – (85/November)
2. Have you seen the weather forecast on TV? – (Yes/warm and sunny/morning/afternoon/scattered showers/occasional thunderstorms)
3. Don't you think it's getting a bit chilly in here? – (close/window)
4. I'm playing tennis with Wanda tomorrow afternoon. – (Well/hope/not rain)
5. Phew, that bag is terribly heavy. – (carry/for you)
6. I'm going for a short walk now. – (come too)
7. Their plane left at 10.30. Now it's twelve o'clock. – (So/be/London/by now)
8. I'm afraid I've lost my purse. – (never/see money/again)
9. I've just heard that there is going to be a printers' strike tomorrow. – (Yes/expect/not be any newspapers/for a few days)

25 *Complete these sentences, using the* will-*future or the present progressive:*

1. My parents . . . with us	stay
for a few days in the	
Christmas holidays.	
2. We . . . to the open air	go
rock festival tonight.	
Do you think the weather	
. . . fine?	stay
3. If I look at the irregular	
verbs again, I . . . all right	be
in the test tomorrow.	
4. . . . you . . . to the swimming-pool this afternoon?	go
– Yes. – Well, you'd	
better leave a note for	
Darrel. Otherwise he . . .	not know
where you are.	
5. I . . . Frank at Susi	meet
Wong's restaurant	
tonight. – Well, I hope	
you . . . a good time.	have
6. The painters have	
just rung up. They say	
they . . . this Thursday. –	come
I . . . that when I see them.	believe
7. I . . . Marion at the	collect
airport tomorrow.	
But I've only got this	
old photo of her. – I'm	
sure that you . . . her	recognize
even so.	
8. My brother . . . on	get married
Saturday. – I hope	
he . . . very happy.	be
9. What, he . . . again	go out
tonight? If he doesn't	
start working a bit harder,	
he . . . his exams at the	not pass
end of term.	
10. We . . . to Scotland	go
this summer. – . . .	fly
you . . .? – No, we . . .	take
probably . . . the car.	

26 *Say what these people will be doing in the summer holidays. Use the future progressive.*

1. Carol – lie on beach – South of France
2. Chuck – tour New England – group of bikers
3. Andrew – take a Spanish course – San Diego
4. The Brundles – repaint holiday home – Amity Island
5. Hank and Brad – take part in beach volleyball tournaments – California
6. Tina – stay at home/save money for skiing holiday – Switzerland
7. Bob – go to summer school
8. Matthew – help parents with the harvest – farm in Oregon
9. Sally – work – local pizza parlour

27 *At church this morning the Reverend I. Deal is painting a picture of heaven. Can you complete the picture? Use the verbs below and the future progressive.*

> drive, enjoy, play (2 ×), not play, quarrel, read, sail, shine, sit, smile, not smoke, wait, wonder

When I get through the pearly gates, St Peter . . . for me. He . . ., and the sun . . .. In the distance, someone . . . a racing car – that'll be my brother, and on a lake behind St Peter my father . . . his yacht. My mother . . . quietly with him and . . . a book. He . . . – that's what killed him. Two of my oldest friends . . . – I'm afraid that's what they enjoy most. On the other side there will be a football stadium, but the teams . . . today and everything will be nice and quiet.
When my family arrive after many years, I . . . the drums for the Heavenly Orchestra. We . . . all . . . "Mr Simpson Goes to Town" very loud, and my family . . . what's going on. Then they'll say: "That must be Dad. No one else likes that tune." And two minutes later, they . . . it too! That's my idea of heaven.

28 *Make sentences with the words in brackets. Use the simple present or the present progressive:*

1. (We – fly – America – next week)
2. (Our plane – leave – Munich airport – 7.30 a.m.)
3. (It – get to – Düsseldorf – 8.30)
4. (We – meet – Susan and Tina – Düsseldorf airport)
5. (Connecting flight – Los Angeles – be – 10.30)
6. (The plane – arrive – Los Angeles – 3.30 – afternoon)
7. (Where – you – stay – Los Angeles?)
8. (We – stay – hotel – near airport)
9. (Thursday July 4th – we – go – Disneyland)
10. (Evening – we – watch – Independence Day fireworks – Disneyland)
11. (What time – fireworks – begin?)
12. (The fireworks – start – 11 p.m. – end – midnight)
13. (Next day – we – drive on – San Diego)

29 *Complete these sentences, using the simple present or the* will-*future*

1. I . . . as soon as I . . . to Glasgow.	telephone get
2. If you . . . in the evening, we . . . to collect you from the station.	arrive be able
3. Mummy . . . you a story before you . . . to bed.	read go
4. Sue . . . little Mark until his parents . . . home.	look after come
5. When she . . ., I . . . her all about it.	ring up tell
6. The ferry to Folkestone . . . at 7 p.m., so we . . . something to eat on board.	leave probably have
7. I expect she . . . very well in her exams if she . . . working so hard.	do go on
8. You . . . your way all right once you . . . to the Minster.	find get
9. They . . . when they . . . the news.	be shocked hear
10. Play . . . as soon as the rain	continue stop

30 *Complete these sentences, choosing the correct verb forms from the three alternatives in brackets. Sometimes there are several solutions. Write down all the solutions which you think are correct.*

1. Can you believe it? Grandmother . . . 89 in October.
(is/will be/is going to be)
2. I hope the Jacksons . . . soon.
(will come/are coming/come)
3. The ferry . . . Weymouth at 7.15 p.m.
(is going to leave/will leave/leaves)
4. What . . . tomorrow at this time?
(will you be doing/are you doing/do you do)
5. Is it really true that Sally and Tim . . . next month?
(get married/will have got married/are getting married)

6. He's got some crazy plans.
   He . . . the Sahara on his bike.
   (will cross/is crossing/is going to cross)
7. So that's been decided now.
   We . . . at 6 tomorrow morning.
   (set off/are setting off/will set off)
8. We expect that the Smiths . . . with us for a few days before they go on to Austria.
   (are staying/stay/will be staying)
9. If you leave the car window open all the time you . . . stiff neck by the end of the trip.
   (will have/will be having/are going to have)
10. I have no idea when the concert . . ..
   (ends/will end/is going to end)

31 *Translate these sentences into English:*

1. Es ist kalt hier. Ich mache das Fenster zu.
2. Vor den Sommerferien kaufe ich mir einen neuen Fotoapparat.
3. Wenn du am Montag ankommst, holen wir dich am Flughafen ab.
4. Mach dir keine Sorgen, ich fahre vorsichtig.
5. Unser Flug geht um 10.30 ab Heathrow.
6. Ich gebe dir das Buch zurück, sobald ich es gelesen habe.
7. Ich hoffe dir gefällt der Film.
8. Ich gehe heute Abend mit Freunden aus. Wir treffen uns um sieben.
9. Wenn wir in London sind, schauen wir uns ein Musical an.
10. Kommt ihr am Mittwoch oder am Donnerstag zurück?

The future perfect

GG 70; GhE 207

32 *Complete the sentences, using the future perfect (simple or progressive) of the following verbs:*

be married, be used up, cost, finish, not finish, leave, live, play

1. I'm exhausted. We . . . for three hours soon.
2. Shall I collect you at five? – That's too early. I . . . my homework by then.
3. Next year we . . . in our house for exactly twenty years.
4. This time next year I . . . my exams.
5. In two years' time the Johnsons . . . for 30 years.
6. Gill will still be at home next summer, but Tim . . . by then.
7. By the time she finishes college, her education . . . $ 50,000.
8. Some forecasts say that by the middle of the 21st century all fossil fuels . . ..

The conditional and the conditional perfect

GG 71; GhE 210

33 *Use the conditional or the conditional perfect to express results and consequences:*

1. If only Susan had worked a little harder before. (not fail exams)
   She wouldn't have failed her exams.
2. Grandpa should get himself some pet. (not feel so lonely)
3. Why don't you get up a little earlier? (not be late for school every morning)
4. If only they had bought tickets before. (not miss "The Carnations")
5. You should perhaps think of getting some job in the summer holidays. (be able to pay for your driving lessons yourself)
6. I wish I had slept better the night before. (feel better in the match against Tom yesterday)
7. Try going for a walk before going to bed. (probably sleep much better)

The sequence of tenses between sentences GG 72; GhE 179–180

34 *Complete these jokes, choosing the most suitable tense and aspect of the given verbs:*

1. "Doctor, every time I . . .	drink
coffee I . . . a stabbing	get
pain in my left eye."	
"Why . . . you . . .	not take
the spoon out of the cup?"	
2. 1st man: "That . . . a	be
ridiculous pair of socks	
you . . ., one . . . blue and	wear be
the other . . . yellow."	be
2nd man: "I	know
And the funny thing . . .	be
I . . . another pair at	have got
home exactly like these."	
3. Voice on telephone:	
"I . . . afraid Alice . . . at	be not be
school today".	
Headmaster: "Who . . .?"	call
Voice: "It . . . my mother."	be
4. "Waiter! Waiter! . . .	be
the pancakes . . . long?"	
"No sir. I . . . they . . .	expect be
round as usual."	
5. "Waiter! . . . you . . .	have
chicken legs?"	
"No sir. I always . . .	walk
like this."	
6. "I . . . my dog."	lose
"Why . . . you . . . an advertisement in the paper?"	not put
"Don't be silly – he can't read."	
7. My dog . . . really stupid.	be
He . . . a bone for three	chew
hours the other day.	
Then he . . . off on the	walk
other three legs.	
8. "Waiter, what soup	
. . . this?"	be
"It . . . bean soup, sir."	be
"I . . . what it . . .,	not care be
I . . . to know what	want
it . . . now."	be
9. Teacher: "If you . . .	have
20 pence and you . . .	ask
your granny for another	
20 and your grandpa	
for 30, what . . . you . . .,	have
John?"	
John: "20 pence, sir."	
Teacher: "You . . .	not know
your arithmetic, young	
man."	
John: "And you . . .	not know
my grandparents, sir."	
10. My granddad . . .	go
to a fortune teller	
the other day.	
She . . .: "You . . . to be	say live
eighty."	
He . . .: "I . . . eighty."	say be
She . . .: "See,	say
I . . . you".	tell
11. Yesterday my sister . . .	do
her homework and she	
. . . my mum for help.	ask
She . . .: "Mum I . . .	say look
for the lowest common	
denominator." *(kleinster gemeinsamer Nenner)*	
My mum . . .: "They	say
should . . . that by now.	find
They . . . for it when	look
I . . . at school."	be
12. My mum . . . out driving	be
the other day when	
she . . . by a policeman.	be stopped
He . . .: "When I . . . you	say see
coming up Market	
Street I . . . fifty-five	think
at least."	
My mum . . .: "Come	say
on, officer, I . . .	not look
as old as that."	
13. My brother . . .	get
to work late one day.	
They . . .:	say
"What . . .?"	happen
He . . .:	say
"I . . .."	oversleep
They . . .: "What? . . .	say sleep
you . . . at home as well?"	

14. When my brother ...	be
a year old, my mother ...	be
very proud of him.	
She ... to the neighbour:	say
"He ... ever since	walk
he ... eleven months old."	be
The neighbour ...:	say
"Poor little thing, he must be tired now."	

The use of tenses in conditional sentences GG 73–75; GhE 215–218

35 *Fill in the correct verb forms to express realistic conditions:*

1. If ... today,	not rain
I ... water the flowers.	have to
2. They ... their train if	miss
they	not hurry
3. If you ... science fiction,	like
you ... this film.	enjoy
4. The neighbours ...	be annoyed
if you ... your car in	park
their drive.	
5. If I ... all those jobs by	finish
this evening, I ... to go	be able
to the cinema.	
6. Sue ... to go to the party	not be able
at the weekend if she	
still ... a temperature.	have
7. If you ... all that way	hike
since breakfast, you ...	be
very tired now.	
8. What ... if you ... the job?	do not get

36 Guiseppe Verdi Smith, the great cook, is giving a cookery class.

What are his tips? Sometimes you can express his advice in different ways:

If you use oven gloves, you won't burn yourself.
If you don't use oven gloves, you may burn yourself.
Use oven gloves and you won't burn yourself / or you may burn yourself.

use oven gloves	–	burn yourself
wear an apron	–	splash your clothes
cover saucepans with a lid	–	waste energy
fry onions slowly	–	burn them
leave oven door closed	–	your cakes/go down in the middle
warm plates	–	food/quickly get cold
use first class food only	–	your recipes/not turn out well

37 *Use conditional sentences to comment on these situations:*

1. Jane doesn't speak Spanish. She won't get the job.
   If Jane spoke Spanish, she would get the job.
2. He doesn't have a lot of money. He can't get himself an expensive car.
3. I'm not English. That's why I can't speak English perfectly.
4. I'm not hungry. I won't order a big meal.
5. We haven't got his address. We can't write him a postcard.
6. I'm not a millionaire. I won't buy you that diamond ring.
7. Jack can't swim. That's why he's so afraid of sailing.
8. We don't have a car. We can't take you home.
9. Linda doesn't love him. That's why she doesn't want to marry him.

38 *What would you do in these situations?*

1. You arrive home and see someone in your house. (ring the police).
   If I arrived home and saw someone in my house, I would ring the police.
2. You get home in the dark and drop your key down a hole. (try to get it out of the hole)

3. You book a holiday cottage with a travel agency. When you get there, you notice that it is occupied by other people. (phone the agency)
4. You want to go on a bike ride but your bike has a flat tyre. (repair it)
5. You have a visitor but you have to go to the shops. (ask the visitor to come along)
6. You buy a radio from a friend. It stops working a week later. (ask for your money back)
7. You like your neighbours but they have their music on loud all day. (ask them to turn it down)
8. You are always late for school because no one in your family ever hears the alarm clock. (buy an extra loud alarm clock)
9. You find a book you borrowed from the library months ago. (take it back as soon as possible)

39 *Say what would (not) have happened if things had been different:*

1. The post came very early that day, so I received Uncle Jack's letter in time.
   If the post had not come so early that day, I wouldn't have received Uncle Jack's letter in time.
2. Uncle Jack offered me a holiday job at the lab, so I didn't leave for France with my friends.
3. As I wasn't on the ferry, I didn't get seasick.
4. The job at the lab was interesting, so I went back there in the next holidays.
5. They were developing a new metal for aircraft engines, so I learnt a lot about metallurgy.
6. I wasn't old enough to work there full time, so Uncle Jack couldn't offer me a full-time job.
7. I worked as many hours as I could, so I earned quite a lot of money.
8. I saved most of it, so I was able to buy myself a motorbike.
9. I had this nasty accident a few weeks later. But on the other hand I met this lovely nurse in hospital.

40 *Connect the two parts that go together to form sensible conditional sentences. Use the conditional or the conditional perfect.*
(If you are less certain, use might *instead of* would.)
Example: 1. If William the Conqueror had not invaded England in 1066, there wouldn't be so many French words in the English language today.

1. If William the Conqueror had not invaded England in 1066,	– the USA still be part of the British Empire
2. If England had not defeated the Great Armada in 1588,	– India not become independent so quickly
3. If the American colonists had been happy to go on paying taxes to England,	– not discover America in 1492
4. If Gandhi had not become such a popular leader in India,	– not be so many French words words in the English language today
5. If Columbus had not sailed west in order to get to China,	– not become the greatest sea power in the world
6. If there had not been any slavery in the Southern States,	– far less pollution today
7. If the USA had not joined the Allies in the 2nd World War,	– people still have to go by ferry today
8. If the automobile had never been invented,	– the Americans not land on the moon in 1969
9. If the Channel tunnel had not been built,	– the war last much longer
10. If the United States had not competed with the USSR during the Cold War,	– the Civil War not take place at all

41 *Translate these sentences into English:*

1. Wenn ich du wäre, würde ich nicht über die Autobahn fahren.
2. Wenn es irgendwelche Schwierigkeiten geben sollte, ruft doch bitte an.
3. Wenn deine Mutter nicht so ängstlich *(anxious)* wäre, würde sie dir erlauben, mit uns zum Zelten zu gehen.
4. Es wäre ganz anders, wenn es gefährlich wäre.
5. Falls wir nicht zu Hause sein sollten, wenn ihr kommt, könnt ihr den Schlüssel bei Eastwoods abholen.
6. Solltet ihr schon am Freitag kommen, könnt ihr die Nacht bei uns bleiben.
7. Falls ihr Hunger haben solltet, findet ihr etwas im Kühlschrank.
8. Sollte der Hund bellen, habt keine Angst. Er beißt nicht.

Past tense and past perfect to express wishes GG 76; GhE 214

42 *Complete these wishes, using the past tense or the past perfect of the verbs on the right:*

1. If only I . . . enough time to read all the books I'm interested in!	have
2. I'd rather you . . . at home for a change tonight.	stay
3. It's high time your mother . . . to your French teacher.	speak
4. If only I . . . the novel before the test!	read
5. I wish you . . . to see us more often.	come
6. If only he . . . so much all the time!	not smoke
7. I wish I . . . those dirty old jeans for the interview yesterday.	not wear
8. If only I . . . that the roads were icy that morning!	know
9. Suppose you . . . Joanna before you married Agatha.	meet
10. I can't see past the man in front of me. I wish I . . . a little taller.	be

43 *Translate these sentences into English.*

1. Wenn du am Ende des Schuljahres nach London fährst, musst du dir unbedingt das Musical „Cats" anschauen.
2. Wenn ich du wäre, würde ich vorher T. S. Eliot's „Old Possum's Book of Practical Cats" lesen.
3. Solltest du es in unserer Buchhandlung nicht bekommen (können), kann ich es dir leihen.
4. Denn wenn du die Katzen aus den Gedichten [bereits] kennst, kannst du die Aufführung noch mehr genießen.
5. Hätte ich die Gedichte selbst vorher gelesen, hätte ich die Songs viel leichter verstanden.
6. Übrigens, wenn du einen guten Platz bekommen willst, solltest du jetzt [schon] telephonisch eine Karte bestellen.
7. Wenn ich doch nur im Juli genügend Zeit hätte, mit dir mitzufahren.
8. Es wäre mir viel lieber, du würdest erst im September fahren.

Chapter 9: The passive voice

The passive forms of the verb
GG 77; GhE 178, 253, 256

1 Sam Fuller, a famous film star, is looking forward to playing the leading role in an action film in Hollywood.
Complete the following sentences using the will-*future (passive form) of the verbs in brackets:*

1. At the airport Sam Fuller . . . by a lot of photographers. (meet)
2. He . . . by top reporters. (interview)
3. He . . . by the director of the film company. (to welcome)
4. He will stay at a wonderful private house. All his expenses . . . by the film company. (pay)
5. His dog . . . by a butler. (look after)
6. Breakfast, lunch and dinner . . . by the chef of a famous restaurant. (prepare)
7. He . . . the studios by the director himself. (show)
8. All the stunts in the film . . . by Sam Fuller himself. (do)

2 *Complete the following sentences by using the present perfect (passive form) of the verbs in brackets:*

1. Your hair . . ., I see. It looks much better now. (cut)
2. All the pears . . .. We've stored them in the garage. (pick)
3. . . . the dustbins . . . yet? (to empty)
4. The escaped convict . . .. He is back in prison now. (catch)
5. I really am worried. All my credit cards . . .. (steal)
6. I'm awfully sorry. The bicycle you wanted to buy . . .. (sell)
7. Little Tibby, our cat, has gone. We've looked for her everywhere! I hope she . . .. (not run over)
8. Your grandfather has had a heart attack. He . . . to hospital. (take)
9. I've come to pick up my bike. – I'm sorry, it . . . yet. (not repair)
10. I'd like to pay my bill, please. – You needn't. It . . . by your friend. (pay)

3 *Complete these sentences by using the present or past progressive (passive form) of the verbs in brackets:*

1. Why can't we watch TV at your house? – Because our TV . . . at the moment. (repair)
2. Two new hotels . . . in our town at the moment. (to build)
3. Why can't we swim in the swimming-pool? – Because it . . .. (clean)
4. Have you heard? The old post office . . . into a disco. (turn)
5. When the architect arrived at the new building, the windows . . .. (put in)
6. I'm sorry, but you can't see the monkeys now. They . . .. (feed)
7. The front door . . . at the moment. Please use the back door. (paint)
8. When we arrived, a big Christmas tree . . . in the town square. (put up)
9. At that moment she realized that she . . . by a strange man. (follow)

4 *Fill in* must, can, should, ought to *or a form of* have to *and a passive infinitive. (Sometimes there are several possibilities.)*

1. After the accident the left headlight of my car . . .. (replace)
2. These dogs are dangerous. They . . . alone. (leave)
3. Little Tibby looks very ill. She . . . to a vet at once. (take)
4. The park looks wonderful. It . . . by a very good landscape gardener. (design)
5. Cars . . . regularly. (check)
6. Yesterday's match . . . because of bad weather. (cancel)
7. The child is seriously ill. She . . . immediately. (operate on)

8. The lift . . . if there's a fire. (not use)
9. The children . . . by a neighbour while their mother was in hospital. (look after)
10. Dogs . . . lots of tricks. (teach)

5 *Complete the sentences by choosing from one of the following verbs. Be careful with the tenses.*

beat, bite, break, break open, build, damage, follow about, hold up, open, show

1. Yesterday I . . . by a dog. Look at my hand!
2. We can't cross the river here. The bridge . . . by the storm.
3. The house . . . in the 19th century.
4. Last night we . . . by a traffic jam.
5. The box had to . . . by force.
6. In the match on Saturday, Manchester . . . by Liverpool. The result was 3 : 0.
7. After the football match a lot of shop windows . . . by so-called football fans.
8. Members of the Royal Family . . . by reporters wherever they go.
9. Next week the new film . . . in British cinemas.
10. The new supermarket in the High Street . . . tomorrow.

6 *Complete the sentences by using a suitable verb in the proper passive form:*

1. Your windows look super. – Well yes, they . . . yesterday.
2. Don't touch the railing. It . . ., and the paint may still be wet.
3. How old is this house? – It . . . in 1950.
4. Your right light is broken. – Yes, I know, it . . . tomorrow.
5. The litter bins . . . every day. But they still always seem to be full.
6. Have you received the parcel yet? – Yes, it . . . just . . ..
7. Are you sure the brakes are all right? – Yes, they . . . yesterday.
8. What a mess! All those clothes out there. – They . . . by the Red Cross.

Passive sentences with and without a *by*-agent GG 78; GhE 58

7 *Form passive sentences using the expressions given and one of the verbs on the right:*

1. Lincoln/Ford's Theatre in Washington
   Lincoln was assassinated in Ford's Theatre in Washington.
2. Martin Luther King/1968
3. Queen Elizabeth/1953
4. The Berlin Wall/1989
5. America/Columbus
6. The Mona Lisa/Leonardo da Vinci
7. Every year/Parliament/the Queen
8. The Magic Flute/Mozart
9. Hamlet/Shakespeare
10. German/Germany, Austria and Switzerland

compose
crown
discover
assassinate
open
paint
pull down
shoot
speak
write

8 *Change the following sentences into the passive. Use the* by-*agent only where it makes sense.*

1. The police arrested the burglar.
2. Sam Fuller plays the leading part in this film.
3. At the police station they took his photo and his fingerprints.
4. In England people eat a lot of sweets.
5. In Japan a lot of businessmen play golf.
6. Someone has stolen my watch.
7. You need wood to produce matches, paper, furniture and many other things.
8. People soon covered the walls with graffiti.
9. Next week the mayor will open the new road.
10. His followers love him and his opponents respect him.

Verbs with prepositions in passive sentences GG 79; GhE 60

9 *Change the following sentences into the passive. Use the* by-*agent only where it makes sense.*

1. Nobody has ever driven on this road before.
   This road has never been driven on before.
2. Her grandmother will look after Susan while her parents are away.
3. When we came back last night, we saw that burglars had broken into our house.
4. Has anybody called for a doctor?
5. The police are searching for the missing child.
6. Can we rely on her?
7. She noticed that people were staring at her.
8. The Bensons' grandson took over the family business.
9. We'll look into every possibility.
10. It isn't nice to feel that everyone is laughing at you.

Verbs with two objects in passsive sentences GG 80; GhE 61

10 *Change the following sentences, using the "personal passive":*

1. They showed me the picture she had painted.
   I was shown the picture she had painted.
2. They showed us a photograph of their baby.
3. The nurse handed the children a box of chocolates.
4. They told him a lot of lies.
5. Nobody took any notice of him.
6. They have offered me a job in advertising.
7. The police offered the public a reward of £ 5,000 for any information leading to the arrest of the terrorists.
8. Their teacher gave them a lot of homework.
9. In a 3-hour operation the doctors gave a 30-year-old man an artificial heart.
10. They sent me a letter by airmail.
11. Somebody gave me a free ticket for "Swan Lake".
12. The waiter handed us the menu.

Passive sentences with verbs of saying and thinking GG 81; GhE 62

11 *Translate the following sentences into German:*

1. A hot bath is said to be very relaxing after sport.
2. The new entrance exams are supposed to test intelligence rather than knowledge.
3. The original inhabitants of Alaska are supposed to have come from Siberia.
4. He is believed to be having an affair with his secretary.
5. The patient was reported to be fit and well.
6. The Prime Minister is supposed to visit New York next week.
7. He was expected to arrive on Tuesday.
8. Some of Shakespeare's plays are said to have been written by other playwrights.
9. New York is said to be one of the most exciting cities in the world.
10. The game of football is thought to have started in the 13th century.

Chapter 10: The auxiliaries

Auxiliaries and main verbs

GG 82; GhE 221

1 Susan thinks Ben is "Mr Wonderful". This is what she says about him:

1. Ben is very clever.
2. He can speak seven languages.
3. He plays in a famous orchestra.
4. And he practises nine hours a day.
5. He has travelled all over the world.
6. He went to Australia last year.
7. He is going to climb Mount Everest next year.
8. He was born in Singapore.
9. His parents live in Hong Kong.
10. His photograph was in Time Magazine two years ago.
11. He knows a lot of important people.
12. He has lunch with the President regularly.

But Ann knows that all this isn't true:
1. He isn't very clever.
Go on. Make Susan's statements negative.

2 *Ask questions about the words in italics. Use the question words* when, where, who, how many, how long, what.

1. Kay must be at school *at 8.45.*
When must Kay be at school?
2. The Millers live *in Los Angeles.*
3. I met *Johnny Carson* at the station last night.
4. We had dinner together *at the Albatross Hotel.*
5. Johnny can speak *five* languages.
6. My grandmother drinks *ten* cups of tea a day.
7. The Thompsons have lived in London *for five years.*
8. They went there *five years ago.*
9. Peter mainly reads *science magazines.*

Be, have and *do* used as auxiliaries and as main verbs

GG 83–85; GhE 243–255

3 *Put in the correct form of* be:

1. He . . . rather stupid, . . . he?
2. Please . . . quiet. I . . . listening to the news.
3. There you . . . at last! I've . . . waiting here for ages.
4. The house has . . . there a long time. I think it . . . built in the last century.
5. What will you . . . doing tomorrow at this time?
6. Last night I . . . going to write a letter, but then I . . . rung up by a cousin of mine, and by the time she had finished it . . . too late to start.
7. The Joneses have . . . members of the club as long as I can remember.
8. While the bridge . . . . . . built last year the traffic had to . . . redirected.
9. What colour . . . your new car?
10. How much . . . these jeans here?
11. What . . . going on over there?
12. Look, the injured player . . . . . . carried from the field.
13. The boss has just rung up. You . . . to ring back as soon as possible.
14. Oh stop it now, you . . . . . . very annoying today.

4 *Translate these sentences into English, using expressions or verb forms with* have *for the words in italics:*

1. Sie *ist* bisher noch nicht in den USA *gewesen.*
2. *Bist* du schon mit den Hausaufgaben *fertig*?
3. Ich *warte schon* seit 14 Tagen auf eine Antwort.
4. Er *hätte* die Fahrprüfung *bestanden,* wenn er nicht so schnell *gefahren wäre.*

5. *Hast* du den ganzen Kuchen *aufgegessen*?
6. Bakers *haben* keine Kinder, aber sie *haben* 7 Katzen.
7. *Besaßen* sie ein eigenes Haus in London, oder *hatten* sie eine Wohnung?
8. Wir *aßen* gerade *zu Mittag*, als sie anriefen.
9. *Viel Spaß* auf der Party.
10. *Nimm* doch noch ein Stück Kuchen.
11. Laß uns mal das Schaufenster *anschauen*.
12. Nach dem Spiel war er so müde, daß er nicht *duschte*, sondern gleich ins Bett ging.

5 *Fill in the correct form of* do:

1. . . . you like badminton? – No, I . . ., but my brother . . ..
2. – He plays football too, . . . he?
3. – Yes, he . . ., and so . . . I.
4. That house . . . look attractive, . . . it?
5. What is she . . .? – She's . . . her homework.
6. – She's been . . . it for hours now.
7. Have you . . . the ironing yet? – No, I must . . . it this afternoon.
8. What are you . . . in the holidays? Are you going away?
9. – No, we aren't. We want to . . . some jobs in the house and in the garden.
10. . . . help yourself – have another sandwich.
11. . . . not walk on the grass.
12. . . . Jimmy ring up last night? – No, he . . .. But I expect he'll . . . so tomorrow.

Now translate the sentences into German.

The modal auxiliaries: syntactic features GG 86; GhE 221

6 *Translate these sentences into English:*

1. Er kann gut Englisch.
2. Es tut mir leid, aber ich muss jetzt nach Hause.
3. Kann ich mir dein Fahrrad leihen?
4. Könntest du mir einen Gefallen tun?
5. Ihr könnt da nicht rein. Die Tür ist abgeschlossen.
6. Ich muss ins Bett, ich glaube ich habe Fieber.
7. Wir hätten früher losfahren sollen.
8. Du hättest mich nicht abzuholen brauchen.
9. Wir dürfen hier nicht so laut sprechen.
10. Sie brauchen uns morgen früh nicht zu wecken. Wir haben einen Wecker.

Can/could GG 88; GhE 223–226

7 *Use* can/could *or a form of* be able to *to complete these sentences. (Sometimes there are several possibilities.)*

1. She . . . swim when she was only three.
2. John expects to . . . afford a trip to New York next spring.
3. I've no idea what he's doing. We (not) . . . contact him since February.
4. The police had to admit that they (not) . . . catch the gangsters in the motorway chase last week.
5. It was so noisy that we (not) . . . understand what was said.
6. Perhaps we . . . go away on holiday this summer.
7. I'm afraid I've lost my way. (you) . . . tell me how I . . . get to the station?
8. This looks very odd. I'm certain it (not) . . . be right.

May/might/mustn't GG 89; GhE 227–228

8 *Use* may/might/may not/mustn't *or a form of* (not) be allowed to *to complete these sentences. (Sometimes there are several possibilities.) Then translate the sentences into German.*

1. We . . . make so much noise. Mum is having a rest.

2. When I was small I . . . eat many sweets.
3. On most flights passengers . . . take 20 kilos of luggage.
4. In Germany people . . . walk on the grass in some parks.
5. The students wanted to know whether they . . . use dictionaries for the translation.
6. When we have children they . . . wear what they like.
7. We . . . stay up so late again. I feel awful this morning.
8. Can you see the lights over there? That . . . be Dover.
9. (I) . . . go home, Mrs Parker? I've got an awful headache. – Yes, of course you . . ..
10. You . . . touch the little birds. Their mother . . . like it.
11. Kate . . . stay out late ever since she was 14.
12. We made such a mess last time that I don't think we . . . have another party for some time.

Must/needn't GG 90; GhE 229

9 *Complete the sentences, using* must/needn't *or a form of* (not) have to *with one of these expressions*:

worry about getting seasick, believe the story, cancel the trip, collect me from the station, drop him from the team, leave, never wait long, pay an entrance fee, take that book back to the library, take the car, take warm jackets, wash them

1. Your jeans look awful. You . . .
2. We . . .. It's very mild today.
3. I really . . .. It has been lying around for weeks now.
4. Well, you . . .. But Guy told me that it was absolutely true.
5. The train won't wait. So we . . ..
6. We wanted to go to France, but Carol fell ill, so we . . ..
7. The beach wasn't far from the hotel. We . . ..
8. There are so many patients today that it's taking unusually long. So far I . . ..
9. If John should play just as badly in the next match, the coach . . ..
10. You . . .. I only have a small bag.
11. We were lucky.
We . . ..
12. If you went through the Channel Tunnel, you . . ..

Will/would GG 91; GhE 235–238

10 *Translate the sentences, using* will/would *or one of the other verbs that correspond to German* wollen (*or* werden). *(Sometimes there are several possibilities.)*

1. Ich glaube nicht, dass sie so viel Geld für ein Auto ausgeben will.
2. Seine Eltern wollen ihn nicht studieren *(go to university)* lassen.
3. Bonzo will immer in der Mitte sitzen.
4. Wir wollten eigentlich früher nach Hause gehen, aber Wilsons wollten uns nicht gehen lassen.
5. Würdest du bitte das Fenster zumachen? Es ist kalt.
6. Wir haben schon immer nach Australien in Urlaub fahren wollen.
7. Ich habe Alan gefragt, ob er mir sein Rennrad leiht, aber er will nicht.
8. Und auch Mike wollte mir seins nicht geben.
9. Sandra erwartet, dass ich ihr nachlaufe, aber das werde ich nicht tun.
10. Was für eine Unverschämtheit! *(What cheek!)* Ich werde mich über Sie beschweren.

Used to GG 92; GhE 239–240

11 *Put one of the verbs in brackets in the simple present or simple past and combine the other one with* used to *or* didn't use to/used not to:

1. The Mackintoshes (live) in Glasgow before they (move) to Leeds.
   The Mackintoshes used to live in Glasgow before they moved to Leeds.
2. When she was at school she (like) getting up early, but now she (not mind).
3. There (be) a butcher's shop at the corner of the street when I (be) a boy.
4. He (like) classical music at all, but now that he knows more about it he (enjoy) it very much.
5. My watch (work) like a dream – but then I (drop) it on a cement floor!
6. They (like) him very much. But when he (leave) them all his money they thought he was wonderful.
7. Before she (have) the twins, she (work) in her parents' restaurant.
8. I never (smoke) a lot, and last year I (give) it up altogether.
9. She (play) so much tennis, but that was before she (meet) Bob.
10. When we were younger we (go skiing) a lot, but now we (be) no longer so keen on it.

Shall/should/ought to/be to corresponding to the German *sollen* GG 93; GhE 231–232

12 *Translate the sentences, using* shall/should/ought to/be to *or* be supposed to *for the German* sollen. *(Sometimes there is more than one solution.)*

1. Soll ich einkaufen gehen?
2. Er soll unheimlich reich sein.
3. Du solltest etwas weniger trinken.
4. Sie sollte eigentlich schon hier sein.
5. Sollen wir mal anrufen und fragen, was los ist?
6. Wir hätten daran denken sollen, daß morgen ein Feiertag ist.
7. Ich fühle mich schrecklich. Ich hätte nicht so viel essen sollen.
8. Das Flugzeug sollte um 10 Uhr starten, aber wegen des Streiks verspätete es sich.
9. Der Direktor hat gesagt, dass wir auf jeden Fall *(definitely)* unsere Pässe mitbringen sollen.
10. Entschuldigung, sind sie Frau Miller? Ich soll diese Blumen [hier] abliefern.

Need and *dare* used as auxiliaries and as main verbs GG 94; GhE 241–242

13 *Complete the sentences, using a form of* need *or* dare *with these expressions*:

ask her, ask him about a rise in salary, blame ourselves, bring all that food, bring mine along, do everything today, fill up the tank, go shopping, go to the doctor's, say anything, take umbrellas

1. There is no milk in the fridge. We really . . ..
2. My boss is always in a bad mood. I . . ..
3. The atmosphere was so tense that nobody . . ..
4. We've still got plenty of petrol, so we . . . for at least another fifty miles.
5. It didn't rain all day. We . . ..
6. My temperature seems to have gone down. I don't think I . . ..
7. You've all got bike pumps, so I . . ..
8. We did everything we could. We . . ..
9. You . . .. Look, we've got masses ourselves.
10. I'd like to go out with Carol. But she's got so many admirers I . . ..
11. There's no hurry, so we . . ..

Chapter 11: The verb and its objects and complements

Verbs without an object and verbs with an object GG 95; GhE 44–45

1 *Complete the following sentences using the correct forms of these verbs:*

lie, lay; rise, raise; sit, set; fall, fell

1. She ... the little child gently down on her bed.
2. The cat ... asleep on the floor when the dog came in.
3. Could you ... the table, please?
4. Stratford ... on the river Avon.
5. Our hens ... eggs all the year round.
6. "... on your side and try to forget your headache", my mother said to me.
7. The sun ... in the east and ... in the west.
8. He ... his eyebrows and looked at us all critically.
9. The sun had already ... when he woke up.
10. When the Speaker came in all the MPs ... from their seats.
11. The policeman ... his hand to stop the traffic.
12. When his wife came in he ... at his desk writing.
13. He carefully ... the tray down on the table.
14. She wiped the bench carefully before she ... on it.
15. When he stumbled on the steps all the plates ... out of his hands.
16. During the reign of Elizabeth I they ... a lot of trees for building ships.
17. The snow ... softly from the grey sky.

2 *Translate the following sentences into English:*

1. Oh nein! Der Hund liegt auf Muttis neuer Jacke.
2. Alle Vögel legen Eier.
3. „Bitte hebt eure Hände, wenn ihr etwas sagen wollt", sagte der Lehrer.
4. Der Fluß ist 50 cm gestiegen.
5. Bitte setzt euch!
6. Ich habe meinen Wecker auf *(for)* 4 Uhr gestellt.
7. Die Statue fiel auf den Boden und zerbrach.
8. Leider mußten einige der alten Bäume gefällt werden.

3 *Translate the following sentences into German:*

1. Animals usually grow faster than humans.
2. They grow a lot of cotton in the southern states of the USA.
3. Liz ran quickly downstairs to welcome her boyfriend.
4. My mother runs her own business.
5. It was terrible! The lifts in the skyscraper did not work.
6. In the 19th century even children had to work machines.
7. We had to walk 5 miles to the nearest petrol station.
8. You ought to walk your dog twice a day.

Phrasal verbs GG 96; GhE 47–48

4 *Fill in the correct prepositions or adverbial particles:*

1. I get ... very well with my father.
2. Have you got ... the shock of your accident?
3. When do you get ... in the morning?
4. Although she was seriously ill she never gave ... hope.
5. Darren made ... the story, but nobody believed it.

6. It was so cold that I put . . . two pullovers under my anorak.
7. Could you put . . . the lights when you go to bed, please?
8. "Can I speak to the manager, please?" – "O.K., I'll put you . . .".
9. We must do the test on Friday. It would not be good to put it . . . till Monday.
10. Since the dog was rather dangerous, they had to put . . . a strong fence.
11. It's a very small room. But we'll have to put . . . . . . it.
12. He rang . . . the police and told them that he needed help.
13. The dog waited patiently . . . its food.
14. I've forgotten my alarm clock. Please wake me . . . at 6 o'clock.
15. "Let's wash these plates . . . straight away", said my mother.

5 *Translate into English, using phrasal verbs:*

1. Katie schlägt ihrem Vater nach.
2. Der Hubschrauber startet gerade.
3. Sie übernimmt immer mehr Arbeit als gut für sie ist.
4. Eine neue Sprache zu lernen nimmt viel Zeit in Anspruch.
5. Jede Woche trägt Bill Zeitschriften aus.
6. Er schaute mich an.
7. Die Krankenschwester kümmerte sich um das Baby.
8. Ich freue mich darauf, dich in London zu treffen.
9. Was suchst du (gerade)?
10. Ich kenne dieses Wort nicht. Ich muss es nachschlagen.

Verbs with two objectes

GG 97; GhE 49–51

6 *Translate into English. Decide whether to use* to *with the direct object or not.*

1. Er bot ihr seinen Stuhl an.
2. Ich würde dich gerne meinen Freunden vorstellen.
3. Bring mir das Buch bitte.
4. Könntest du ihm diesen Brief bringen?
5. Der Satz ist ziemlich lang. Ich diktiere ihn euch.
6. Der Lehrer erklärte den Schülern die Bedeutung des Wortes.
7. Tim bot seiner Mutter einen Apfel an.
8. Kannst du mir deinen Kugelschreiber leihen?
9. Hast du Julie gegenüber unser Telefongespräch erwähnt?
10. Herr Webster versuchte, der Polizei den Dieb zu beschreiben.

7 *Complete the following sentences using* say *or* tell:

1. I beg your pardon, what did you . . .?
2. Are you sure you . . . the truth?
3. "Come in", he . . .
4. On my birthday lots of friends came up to . . . hello.
5. Could you . . . me your name, please?
6. He . . . me that he was a fireman.
7. Please don't . . . a word to anybody about what I . . . you.
8. She . . . me the story of her life.
9. I was . . . that she is very pretty.
10. I . . . her what the doctor had . . . to me.

Verbs with object + object complement

GG 98; GhE 57

8 *Translate the following sentences into English, choosing from these verbs:*

appoint, choose, find, look upon, make, regard, take, think

1. In Texas machte das Öl eine Menge Leute reich.
2. Ich halte ihn für einen guten Manager.
3. Ich finde diesen Artikel langweilig.
4. Sie ernannten ihn zum Mannschaftsführer des Teams.
5. Der Maler betrachtete das Bild als sein Meisterstück.

6. Unglücklicherweise hielt die Polizei meinen Freund für einen Drogenhändler.
7. Die Arbeiter wählten Mike zu ihrem Sprecher.
8. Viele Leute halten Bungeespringer für verrückt.
9. Sie erkannten ihn sofort als ihren Anführer an.

Verbal expressions for German adverbs GG 99; GhE 287

9 *Translate the following sentences into English, using verbal expressions for the German adverbs:*

1. Er liest gern Zeitschriften.
2. Ich kann Ihnen leider nicht zustimmen.
3. Hoffentlich kannst du kommen.
4. Die Schüler werden die Geschichte wahrscheinlich kennen.
5. Ich war zufällig im Haus, als das Feuer ausbrach.
6. Sie kommen vermutlich um 4 Uhr zurück.
7. Obwohl die Studenten gebeten wurden ruhig zu sein, sprachen sie einfach weiter.
8. Ich arbeite nicht gern im Garten. Ich sitze lieber an meinem Schreibtisch.
9. Sie wird bestimmt rechtzeitig ankommen.
10. Sein Angebot ist anscheinend das beste.

Chapter 12: The infinitive

Forms and functions of the infinitive GG 100; GhE 256–257, 263 A2

1 *Fill in the correct form of the infinitive – with or without* to, *active or passive. Choose from these verbs:*

be (2×),	build,	do (2×),	fight,	
go (2×),	have,	join,	leave,	pay (2×),
play,	practise,	repair,	see,	stay,
take,	work			

1. Sheila wants ... a stewardess. But her parents want her ... to university.
2. Paul can ... the violin very well, but he must ... an awful lot if he wants ... a good orchestra.
3. The new coach makes his players ... very hard during the week. But after matches he lets them ... out and ... a glass of beer.
4. I think I'd rather ... at home in this awful weather. But if you insist on a walk, we'd better ... an umbrella.
5. I'm sorry I couldn't ... my homework yesterday, but I'll ... able ... it today.
6. Where is Jenny? – No idea, she seems ....
7. The prisoners were made ... a high wall.
8. The accident was so bad that the car couldn't ....
9. This bill ought ... ages ago. You really should ... it last month.
10. Whether the new government will really ... organized crime remains ....

The infinitive construction with *for*
GG 102; GhE 260

2 *Connect these sentences, using infinitive constructions with* for:

1. This letter must arrive by Friday. That is very important.
   It is very important for this letter to arrive by Friday.
2. The box is far too heavy. I can't carry it.
3. We've left some food in the fridge. You can eat it.
4. Peggy is late. That's rather unusual.
5. The food is too hot. Bonzo won't be able to eat it.
6. I've been waiting here for half an hour. But nobody has come and helped me.
7. This is an interesting book. You can read it in the holidays.
8. The noise of the waterfall was too loud. Sherlock Holmes was unable to hear the shot.
9. Helen will be working full time next month. She won't find that easy.
10. Nobody will get all the answers right in the test. I think that is impossible.
11. They will send some sandwiches from the delicatessen. I've arranged that.
12. Is there enough champagne – so that everyone can have a glass?

The infinitive after verbs expressing a wish or intention, and after verbs expressing commands or requests, advice or warnings
GG 101, 103, 104; GhE 264–265

3 *Rewrite the following sentences, using the pronouns and verbs in brackets followed by an "object + infinitive" construction.*

1. Shall I set the table? (you – want)
   Do you want me to set the table?
2. The guide said to the tourists: "Mind the step!" (he – warn)
   He warned them to mind the step.
3. You must meet Tony. (I – would like)
4. The doctor said to the patient: "You really ought to stop smoking, John." (he – advise)
5. Her parents said: "Please don't be late, Chris." (they – not want)
6. The teacher said to the students: "Please do excercises 9 and 10." (she – want)
7. Her mother said to Katie: "You must stay at home with that terrible cold." (she – tell)
8. I'm sure my parents will be back home before supper. (I – expect)
9. The attendant said to the children in the art gallery: "Don't touch the pictures, children." (he – warn)
10. Jim said to his girlfriend: "Could you pay the bill, please?" (he – ask)

4 *Translate these sentences into English, using infinitive constructions:*

1. Dr. Simpson hat George geraten, ein paar Tage im Bett zu bleiben.
2. Er erwartet, dass George sich schnell erholen wird. *(make a quick recovery)*
3. Er möchte aber, dass George nächste Woche noch einmal in seine Praxis kommt.
4. Er hat ihm gesagt, dass er dreimal am Tage zwei „Fluex" Tabletten nehmen soll.
5. George hofft, dass er bald wieder auf sein wird.
6. Er hat die Absicht, bald wieder mit dem Training anzufangen.
7. Aber Dr. Simpson will, dass George erst wieder völlig gesund wird.
8. Er möchte, dass George vorsichtig ist und hat ihn davor gewarnt, unnötige Risiken einzugehen. *(take unnecessary risks)*

The infinitive after verbs of causing or allowing
GG 105; GhE 283, 285

5 *Rewrite these sentences, using* let *or* make + *infinitives.*

1. Higher temperatures will cause the level of the oceans to rise.
   Higher temperatures will make the level of the oceans rise.
2. This government can't permit taxes to go up even further.
3. "You can sit at the front if you like, Dave," said Mr Miller. *Mr Miller . . . Dave . . .*
4. Her parents allowed Joan to stay out until midnight.
5. "You must all use pens. Don't write with biros, children", said the teacher. *The teacher . . .*
6. "That's O.K. with me. You can have the car whenever you want, Sarah", said her father. *Her father . . .*
7. You have to go slow here with all these speed limits. *All these speed limits . . .*
8. The comedian was frightfully funny. I laughed so much! *The comedian . . .*
9. I mustn't forget to post that letter. *Don't . . . me . . .*
10. Mr Dane said: "I can't understand a word of the news. Do turn the volume of that music down in your room, Sam!" *Mr Dane . . .*
11. The heavy snow forced motorists to drive more slowly.

The infinitive after verbs of perception and observation

GG 106; GhE 281–282

6 *Translate these sentences, using the verbs* see, hear, feel, notice *followed by an infinitive:*

1. Es muss Mitternacht gewesen sein, aber Gwendolyn hörte die Kirchenuhr nur einmal schlagen.
2. Dann hörte sie, wie jemand die Treppe heraufkam und vor ihrer Tür anhielt.
3. Sie bemerkte, wie jemand die Tür öffnete und sah, wie der Luftzug *(draught)* die schweren Vorhänge *(curtains)* bewegte.
4. Sie hörte, wie Schritte auf sie zukamen und fühlte, wie ihr Herz schneller schlug.
5. Dann fühlte sie, wie etwas eisig Kaltes ihren Hals berührte.
6. Sie sah, wie eine riesige weiße Gestalt sich kurz *(for a moment)* über sie beugte *(bend)*.
7. Dann sah sie zwei grüne Augen, die sie plötzlich anstarrten.
8. Sie schrie [auf] und sah, wie die Gestalt aus dem Zimmer rannte.
9. Dann hörte sie, wie jemand eine Autotür zuschlug *(slam)* und hörte, wie ein Motor startete und ein Wagen wegfuhr.
10. Am nächsten Morgen, als sie der Polizei den Diebstahl *(theft)* ihres wertvollen Schmuckes *(jewels)* meldete, sagte der Manager des „Haunted Hotel", dass niemand beim Betreten oder Verlassen des Hotels gesehen oder gehört worden sei.

The infinitive after question words

GG 107; GhE 290–291

7 *Use infinitives after question words to sum up what these people are saying or thinking:*

1. "Shall I wear my hair long or short?" Joan wondered.
   Joan wondered whether to wear her hair long or short.
2. "Who should I invite to my birthday party?" Derek wondered.
3. "Where on earth can I park my car?" Judy had no idea.
4. "Do you think I should wear a tie or not?" Dad could not make up his mind.
5. "Do we have to go left or right at the next crossing?" Helen didn't know.
6. "How am I to find the place without a map?" Dick was wondering.
7. "Which book shall I read first – the thriller or the love story?" Rosemary could not decide.
8. "When ought I to be at the airport?" Tim didn't quite know.
9. "What shall I get for Mum's birthday?" Sarah couldn't think.

Infinitives instead of relative clauses with modal auxiliaries, and after *the first, the last,* etc.

GG 108, 109; GhE 300.2

8 *Use infinitive constructions to shorten these statements:*

1. Joanna and Mark left the party at 3 o'clock. They were the last guests.
   Joanna and Mark were the last (guests) to leave the party.
2. If you want to have a fantastic holiday, go to Australia. That is the ideal place.
3. Sir Edmund Hillary reached the top of Mount Everest in 1953. No one had managed to do that before.
4. Pete and Alex didn't understand the joke. They were the only ones.
5. If you want to have a sleepless night, watch the film "Psycho" before you go to bed.
6. The Americans landed on the moon in 1969. They were the first.
7. If you want to know more about Chinese cooking, you must buy the book "Peking Duck".
8. I can't open this parcel. Can you give me some scissors, please?
9. People often remember old friends at Christmas. That seems to be the best time.

The infinitive to express a purpose

GG 110; GhE 296

9 *Connect the two parts that go together to form sensible sentences:*

1. The American tourists had to hurry	a) in order to avoid the cow-pats. *(Kuhfladen)*
2. After dinner, everybody walked down the path	b) to open the wine bottle.
3. We must look more closely at the facts	c) to make life easier for people in wheelchairs.
4. A large number of people had come to the pop festival	d) to admire the garden.
5. The Home was designed	e) to hear the "Boomtown Brats" perform.
6. When I'm in Edinburgh I could use the time between meetings	f) to check the children's mathematical ability.
7. You shouldn't use a screwdriver	g) to buy a new car.
8. Agatha walked across the field very carefully	h) in order to answer that question correctly.
9. These tests have been specially worked out	i) in order to get to the next place on their tour schedule. *(Programm)*
10. We used all the money	j) to look round the city.

The infinitive to express a comment

GG 111; GhE 298

10 *Translate the following "speech" into German, paying particular attention to the infinitive constructions:*

1. To begin with this evening, ladies and gentlemen, I'd like to introduce myself.
2. My name's Reginald Winterbottom, and I'm the man to vote for in the coming elections.
3. My party wants me to win this constituency *(Wahlkreis)*, and, with your help, that's exactly what I intend to do.
4. To be honest with you people, I've been warned to expect tough opposition. *(Widerstand)*
5. But, to put things quite plainly, this is not the time to be afraid of anyone or anything.
6. To tell you the truth, it was the Conservatives that made people suffer during the last four years.

7. And many of you may well have wondered where this country was going and whether ever to trust *(Vertrauen schenken)* politicians' promises again.
8. Well, to cut a long story short, let me tell you that I know what line to take.
9. And, to sum up, I will be the first Labour candidate to win this constituency.
10. We'll work hard to see Britain on top again, and we'll do everything we can to keep her there. Thank you!

Chapter 13: The gerund

The gerund as the subject of a sentence
GG 112; GhE 257.1

1 *Complete the sentences using the following verbs:*

collect, go, learn, listen, read, smoke, walk, watch, work

1. ... cigarettes can be a danger to your health.
2. I don't think ... stamps is an interesting hobby.
3. ... English books is a good way to improve your vocabulary.
4. To me ... to the radio is more relaxing than ... TV.
5. ... can be faster than ... by car during the rush hour.
6. ... a poem by heart can help you to understand it better.
7. ... on an assembly line must be very tiring.

The gerund with a subject of its own
GG 113; GhE 259, 261

2 *Translate the following sentences into German:*

1. Mr Hutchinson was against his daughter getting married so young.
2. You can always rely on Susan doing the right thing.
3. The policeman insisted on him showing his driving licence.
4. Mr Brown was tired of his colleague always using his computer.
5. Susan was ashamed of her brother telling such lies.
6. They are used to their children being rather noisy.
7. Mr Smith was proud of his son Daniel doing so well at university.
8. Nobody will prevent you from doing overtime.
9. I hope you don't mind me coming so early.
10. The applicant had nothing against the manager asking personal questions.

3 *Connect these sentences, using gerund constructions:*

1. I'd like to smoke. Do you mind?
   Do you mind me smoking?
2. She took all the magazines to her room. No one objected.
3. Tom played his trumpet all afternoon. The neighbours disliked it.
4. I drive my father's car sometimes. He doesn't mind.
5. Grandma got up at 5 o'clock every morning. Our family was used to it.
6. I failed the exam. My parents were very disappointed about it.

7. Mr Green watches TV all the time. His wife hates it.
8. We had to shut our books. Our teacher insisted on it.
9. People always ask him for money. He hates it.
10. Our neighbours cut down the old oak tree. We were sorry about that.

Gerund and infinitive after certain verbs
GG 114–115; GhE 271, 275 A, 276

4 *Put in suitable gerunds or infinitives. (Sometimes there are several solutions.)*

1. When the children saw the clown, they started . . . .
2. Please open your books at page 20 and begin . . . the text.
3. Have you finished . . . your letter?
4. I'm afraid we can't drive you to the airport. – That's all right. I don't mind . . . by bus.
5. It's hot in here. Would you mind . . . the window?
6. Our friends suggested . . . the holidays in France.
7. I enjoy . . . the newspaper in the evening.
8. My friend likes . . . out new computer programmes.
9. Susan prefers . . . black and white photos.
10. What would you like . . . ? Tea, coffee, orange juice?
11. I hate . . . the dishes.
12. The children couldn't stand . . . the same games every day.
13. Susan liked . . . at herself in the mirror, especially when she was wearing a new kind of make-up.
14. I'd love . . . to your birthday party, but we're visiting my grandparents at the weekend.

5 *Gerund or infinitive? Put in the correct forms of the verbs in brackets:*

1. When the headmaster came in, we all stopped . . . . (talk)
2. When he got to the post office, he stopped . . . some stamps. (buy)
3. Please remember . . . to the butcher's. We need some sausages. (go)
4. The policeman remembered . . . the photograph before. (see)
5. I'll never forget . . . my way in town as a child. (lose)
6. They left in such a hurry that they completely forgot . . . the front door. (lock)
7. It was cold outside, and we regretted . . . our coats in the coach. (leave)
8. We regret . . . you that your application has not been accepted. (inform)
9. I tried . . . on my book, but there was too much noise. (concentrate)
10. She tried . . . an aspirin, but it didn't help. (take)

The gerund after verb/adjective/noun + preposition
GG 116–118; GhE 269–271, 289

6 *Put in the correct preposition and a gerund. Use the verbs in brackets.*

1. All the boys in my class were crazy . . . football. (play)
2. This factory is famous . . . the best cloth in the area. (produce)
3. Alan has always been good . . . landscapes. (paint)
4. Unfortunately my friend is hopeless . . . . (act)
5. Mary is keen . . . our school rock group. (join)
6. Mr King was tired . . . with his neighbour. (quarrel)
7. My grandma was always afraid . . . her umbrella. (forget)
8. Jack and Toby were ashamed . . . so badly at Catherine's birthday party. (behave)
9. He was proud . . . the race. (win)

10. My aunt is rather fond ... pictures of the royal family. (cut out)
11. We are used ... together. (work)
12. Would you be interested ... on a boat trip down the Thames? (go)

7 *Put in the correct preposition and a gerund. Choose from these verbs:*

be, be given, find, get, get married, go, pay, see, unlock

1. He's always dreamed ... a pilot.
2. The director of the museum is thinking ... to Norway for a few months.
3. After trying for five minutes, I finally succeeded ... the door.
4. We are looking forward ... you again.
5. Has Robert still got the same girlfriend? – Yes, they are talking ... next spring.
6. My aunt insisted ... for her meal, although we had invited her to be our guest.
7. If you don't book very early, you can't rely ... a ticket.
8. Sarah complained ... the smallest room in the hotel.
9. My brother has been offered a job in London. But he is worrying ... a flat there.

8 *Gerund or infinitive? Put in the correct form. Sometimes both forms can be used. Choose from these verbs:*

ask, cook, find, learn, meet, run, win

1. Do you think we've got a chance ... the match?
2. This party will give you the opportunity ... a lot of interesting people.
3. There are many different ways ... meat.
4. Don't worry. There's no danger ... out of petrol.
5. We had no difficulty ... my friend's house.
6. I don't like the idea ... those people for help.
7. The best method ... a language is living among people who speak it.

Preposition + gerund as an adverbial
GG 119; GhE 295

9 *Connect the following sentences (or sentence parts), using gerund constructions introduced by the prepositions in brackets:*

1. Tom came back from school and did his homework. (after)
   After coming back from school, Tom did his homework.
2. Mark tried hard, but he failed his exam. (in spite of)
3. The little boy found and returned the purse. He expected a reward. (for)
4. Mr Turner heard the news and left at once. (on)
5. He checked the oil and the tyres. Then he drove off. (before)
6. The children sold souvenirs to tourists. They earned a lot of money. (by)
7. Rachel left the room. She didn't say a word. (without)
8. A lot of people look round duty free shops, but don't buy anything. (without)
9. Mike Brown is an excellent actor. He is also a good singer and dancer. (apart from)
10. Mr Stevenson leads the choir. He conducts the orchestra too. (as well as)
11. Kay didn't help us with the cleaning but played video games all day. (instead of)

The gerund after expressions like *it's no use, there's no, what about*
GG 120; GhE 263, 275 A

10 *Replace the underlined sentences or clauses by gerund constructions introduced by these expressions:*

what about / how about, it's no use / it's no good, there's no, it's (not) worth

1. Our dog has been missing for two days. – Why don't you put an ad in the paper?
2. You needn't wait for the bus. It has already left.
3. This film is really good. You must go and see it.
4. You never know what may happen if children play at the roadside.
5. Don't post your letter here. The postman has already emptied the letterbox.
6. Last night the TV programme was very poor. It was a waste of time to watch it.
7. Nobody can tell how it will end.
8. What shall we do on Sunday? – We could go for a bike ride.
9. You won't make things any better if you complain. They can't do anything about it.
10. My suitcase is very heavy. Shall we take a taxi?

Chapter 14: Participles

Forms and functions of participles
GG 121; GhE 256, 257.2

1 *Fill in the correct form of the participle. Use the verbs in brackets.*

1. He talked to me for a while and watched me ... the hedge. (cut)
2. One of the cars ... in the getaway was soon found by the police. (use)
3. Jimmy invited us to look at a video about Alaska ... by one of his Eskimo friends. (make)
4. At Clarke's Garage, Vera, ... for her car to be ready, watched the tyres ... . (wait – change)
5. The classrooms looked much better, ... newly ... during the summer holidays. (decorate)
6. The castle, completely ... in the Civil War, was rebuilt in the 18th centrury. (destroy)
7. We noticed lots of fences ... to prevent deer from crossing the road. (put up)
8. The ... machine had to be repaired at once. (damage)
9. When ... up the cliffs, you have a fantastic view of the town below. (walk)
10. Have you left the oven on? I can smell something ... in the kitchen. (burn)
11. The Queen, ... by the Speaker, entered Parliament. (follow)
12. ... so many fantastic films about New Zealand, the Millers were very much looking forward to their holiday there. (see)
13. ... to find the safe, the burglar looked behind all the pictures. (hope)
14. ... such a lovely supper for the two of them, Adam felt disappointed when Eve rang up from her office ... that she had to put in some overtime. (cook – say)
15. ... by dozens of police, the gangsters put down their weapons and gave themselves up. (surround)
16. After the explosion, all the ... workers were taken to hospital immediately. (injure)
17. Whose is that car ... in our drive? (park)

The participle after verbs describing a position or movement

GG 122; GhE 279–280

2 *Translate the following sentences, using the following verbs and participles:*

stand, go, sit, remain, lie, come, stay, leave

1. Er stand an der Bushaltestelle und wartete.
2. Sie blieb auf der Parkbank sitzen, obwohl es angefangen hatte zu regnen.
3. Sie saßen und schauten dem Sonnenaufgang zu.
4. Die Katze und der Hund standen [da] und starrten sich neugierig an.
5. Nach dem Kampf lag der Boxer erschöpft auf seinem Hotelbett.
6. Die Polizisten kamen um die Ecke gelaufen.
7. Fred setzte sich sofort hin, aber seine Frau blieb stehen.
8. [Nur] sehr wenige Gebäude blieben *(be left)* nach dem Erdbeben stehen.
9. Seine zwei Hunde kamen auf ihn zugelaufen, als er nach Hause kam.
10. Der Geheimagent blieb hinter einer Gruppe von Bäumen versteckt.
11. Die Fabrik wird diese Woche wegen des Streiks geschlossen bleiben.

Participles after verbs of perception and observation

GG 123; GhE 281–282

3 *Complete these sentences. Decide whether to use an infinitive or a participle. Choose from these verbs:*

burn, carry, crawl, dig, drive, enter, hide, hold, kick, ring, set, talk, touch

1. We heard Sarah ... to a neighbour but couldn't understand a word of what she was saying.
2. Did you hear the doorbell ... just now?
3. We watched the heavy safe ... to the truck.
4. The revolver was found ... in the freezer downstairs.
5. Are Judy and Tim in love? I noticed them ... hands all through the English lesson.
6. The bankrobbers were last seen ... a green van up the M1 north of York.
7. We walked past the house and noticed John ... an enormous hole in his garden.
8. They were sitting on the beach, watching the sun gradually ... on the horizon.
9. Help! I can feel something funny ... up my back.
10. While he was on the telephone, he smelt something ... in the kitchen.
11. In the crowded Underground Carol suddenly felt someone ... her arm.
12. Well, you needn't say it wasn't you. I **saw** you ... the ball through the window.
13. Nobody has been seen ... the house for days.

Participles and infinitives after verbs of causing and allowing

GG 124; GhE 283–286

4 *Translate these sentences into English, using* have, leave, let *or* make *for German* lassen:

1. Wir hatten es eilig. Aber er ließ uns nicht gehen.
2. Die Lehrerin ließ uns alle unregelmäßigen Verben aufschreiben.
3. Rocky Stewart will [sich] eine 10-Millionen-Dollar Villa in Beverly Hills bauen lassen.
4. Sie schloss die Tür und ließ uns draußen im Regen stehen.
5. Wann hast du dein Auto waschen lassen?

6. Verdammt! Jetzt habe ich meine Tennisschuhe zu Hause gelassen.
7. Es ist furchtbar warm. Bitte lass das Fenster offen.
8. Weißt du, wie dieser Videorecorder funktioniert? – Lass mich [mal] probieren.
9. Sandra lässt sich immer von ihrer Mutter die Haare schneiden.
10. Lass die Kinder nicht auf die Straße laufen.
11. Hinterlasst das Badezimmer so, wie ihr es vorgefunden habt.
12. Die Polizei hielt alle Autos an und ließ die Fahrer aussteigen und ihre Papiere zeigen. Dann ließ sie sie weiterfahren.
13. Wir haben uns die Pflanzen aus Holland schicken lassen.

Participles instead of relative clauses

GG 125; GhE 300–301

5 *Rewrite the following sentences, changing the participle constructions into relative clauses:*

1. "Lord of the Flies", first published in 1954, is a book widely read in schools.
   "Lord of the Flies", which was first published in 1954, is a book which/that is widely read in schools.
2. It was perhaps the novel most discussed in the 1960s.
3. Everyone reading the book will be shocked by the realistic description of human behaviour.
4. The author, William Golding, places a group of small boys, aged between 6 and 12, on a tropical island somewhere in the Pacific.
5. The group are the victims of an atomic war raging *(wüten)* somewhere else.
6. During this war an aircraft carrying this group of English schoolboys crash-lands on the coral island.
7. At first, the children, left on their own without any adults, enjoy themselves on the island.
8. Ralph, chosen as their leader, is an honest boy of average intelligence.
9. He realizes that the first tasks *(Aufgaben)* confronting them are to build shelters *(Schutzhütten)* and to light a fire.
10. But the children building the shelters and looking after the fire soon lose interest in these jobs and run off to play.
11. Gradually tensions *(Spannungen)* develop, breaking out into conflicts, and fears of a "beast" living on the island keep the children awake at night.
12. One night two boys see something looking like the "beast".
13. But they are too frightened to realize that the "beast" is only a dead pilot caught among the rocks and moving up and down in the wind.
14. Ralph, still believing in rules and civilized behaviour, is left by most of the boys.
15. Jack, promising to hunt and kill the "beast", becomes the new leader.
16. The boys following their new leader paint their faces and become "hunters".
17. The boys are no longer children playing games but have become dangerous savages *(Wilde)*.
18. Finally Ralph, hunted down by Jack and his followers, tries to run away like an animal.
19. A fire lit by the hunters destroys most of the island.
20. At the end of the novel, a warship landing at the island takes the survivors away.

Participle constructions as adverbials

GG 126; GhE 292–294

6 *Use participles to shorten these sentences or to connect two sentences:*

1. When we drove past the old church, we noticed that there was a strange light inside.
   (When) driving past the old church, we noticed that there was a strange light inside.

2. Joe had set the table, lit the candles and opened a bottle of wine. Then he waited for the bell to ring.
3. The old tiger had become too dangerous. It had to be killed.
4. All the passengers were on deck. They took photos and made video films of the icebergs.
5. The President slowly walked down the gangway. He was followed by his bodyguards.
6. As she had lived in New York for many years, Sally had got used to the constant noise of police sirens.
7. Though the money had been hidden so cleverly, it was soon discovered by a police dog.
8. While Harriet was staying with her uncle in San Diego, she went across the border to Mexico for a day.
9. As they did not want to give the match away so easily, Spurs fought back in the second half.
10. Eric failed the entrance exam for the second time. He decided to give up.
11. Julia has applied for a summer school course in France. She wants to improve her French.
12. The climber had never been in such a dangerous situation before. So he did not know what to do for a moment.
13. When he did not find anyone to play with, John drove back home from the club.
14. The injured driver was so badly shocked by the accident that he couldn't say a word.
15. Amanda Mondano was surrounded by reporters, photographers and hundreds of fans. She was unable to get into the waiting car.
16. We looked at the map and decided to drive back in the direction we had come.
17. As they had forgotten the tickets for the musical, they were not allowed to enter the theatre.
18. When he had finished the painting, Art Walden stood back to admire it.
19. As they were tired after the long day, the children fell asleep at once.

7 *The following sentences are wrong because the implicit subject of the participle construction is different from that of the main clause. Use adverbial clauses to correct the sentences.*

1. Walking across the farmyard, two eggs fell out of the farmer's basket.
   When the farmer walked across the farmyard, two eggs fell out of his basket./When he walked . . ., two eggs fell out of the farmer's basket.
2. Looking up at the sky, a UFO flew over my head.
3. Though having been repaired only recently, Tim can't rely on his watch at all.
4. While having breakfast, the telephone rang.
5. After finishing my lunch, the waiter gave me the bill.
6. Driving round the corner, the snowball hit the police car.
7. Getting into my car, the milk bottle fell on the ground.
8. Having bitten the postman, the Wilsons kept their dog on a chain.
9. Having paid all her bills, her account at the bank was overdrawn.
10. Having listened to the news again, the politician's speech suddenly became understandable.

Participle constructions with subjects of their own GG 127; GhE 292.1, 294

8 *Translate these sentences into German:*

1. The wind being so terribly strong, the ferry could not leave the harbour.
2. With so many new roads being built in this area, it is difficult to find one's way around.

3. The roads being icy and the mountain passes covered in snow, the rally drivers found it impossible to keep within their time limits.
4. The ski instructor led the way through the fog, his students following behind as well as they could.
5. With all that noise going on next door, I can't concentrate on my homework.
6. It will be a cold night again, with snow falling in some parts of the country.
7. With so many pistes closed for lack of snow, there will be crowds of skiers in the higher parts of the mountains.
8. Conditions not having improved at all in the last few years, the situation in some developing countries is as bad as it was 20 years ago.
9. With so many people unemployed, government spending will rise enormously this year.
10. With the Italians playing such perfect volleyball, the Russians are finding it very difficult to keep their heads above water.

Chapter 15: Subordinate clauses

Adverbial clauses GG 129; GhE 317

1 *Fill in a suitable conjunction of time, place or direction, choosing from the following:*

after, as soon as, before, since, until, when, whenever, where, wherever, while

Sometime there are several possibilities.

1. George has been wearing glasses . . . he was three.
2. The postman waited . . . my mother had locked the dog in . . . he came through the garden.
3. . . . he had eaten three pieces of cake and drunk two milkshakes, he began to feel sick.
4. . . . Marylin Monroe went, there were crowds of people asking for her autograph.
5. We insist on talking to the manager. We won't leave . . . we have seen him.
6. Mark tried on ten pairs of shoes . . . he could decide which ones to buy.
7. I put up the notice . . . everybody could see it.
8. We went in . . . the doors opened.
9. My aunt brings us a present . . . she visits us.
10. It's too noisy to talk in here. Let's go . . . it's a bit quieter.
11. . . . we arrived at the party, most of the other guests had already left.
12. . . . Sandra was looking for her key, somebody opened the door from the other side.

2 *Translate the following sentences into English:*

1. Du kannst die Zeitung haben, sobald ich sie gelesen habe.
2. Bevor er ging, drehte er die Heizung ab.
3. Mein Vater singt oft, während er im Garten arbeitet.
4. Wir müssen warten, bis der Regen aufhört.
5. Immer wenn ich ihn sehe, ist er in Eile.
6. Was hast du gemacht, seit wir uns das letzte Mal trafen?
7. Nachdem sie ihr Gepäck abgeholt hatten, nahmen sie ein Taxi in die Innenstadt.

8. Die Polizei schritt erst ein *(take action)*, als die Hooligans anfingen [mit] Flaschen zu werfen.
9. Er freute sich sehr, als wir ihn besuchten.

3 *Connect these sentences, using one of the following conjunctions:*

although, as, because, even though, since, though, whereas

Sometimes there are several possibilities.

1. They had not arrived in time, so I left a message at the information desk.
   As/Since they had not arrived in time, I left a message at the information desk. / I left a message at the information desk because they had not arrived in time.
2. It was rather cold, but Toby took off his pullover.
3. I hate chips, but my sister loves them.
4. Mary felt very embarrassed. Everybody was looking at her.
5. It was raining, but we had to take the dog out.
6. I like children. They are a nuisance sometimes, though.
7. Mr Miller was elected president. He was the best candidate.
8. She earns a lot of money. Her husband is unemployed.
9. Kevin was not admitted to the film. He was too young.
10. Humans soon get tired of doing the same job again and again. A machine never loses patience.

4 *Fill in a suitable conjunction, choosing from the following:*

as if, as though, even if, if, so . . . that, so that, such . . . that, unless, when

Sometimes there are several possibilities.

1. Although she had only played a small part in the film, she behaved . . . she was a famous film star.
2. I would never buy myself a fur coat, . . . I could afford it.
3. He was . . . exhausted . . . he fell asleep over his meal.
4. He stared at me . . . he had never seen me before.
5. Let's leave in good time . . . we get good tickets for the circus.
6. Follow the green signs at the customs, . . . you have goods to declare.
7. There were . . . a lot of people . . . I didn't see you at first.
8. . . . you put too much tea in the pot, the tea will taste bitter.
9. . . . Dad comes home from work, he is always very hungry.
10. I can make you some sandwiches . . . you're hungry.
11. We always take too much luggage . . . we go on holiday.
12. You needn't come before eight, . . . you want to help us with the preparations.
13. . . . you don't like him, you must admit that he's a good actor.

Defining and non-defining relative clauses

GG 130, 134; GhE 308, 310, 311.2

5 *Add commas where necessary:*

1. Chemistry is the only subject that I find really interesting.
2. Spanish which was our third language was never really popular at our school.
3. Not everything that you read in the papers is really true.
4. "Ben Hur" was one of the longest films that have ever been produced in Hollywood.
5. Mary often plays with her little dog which she calls Fluffy.
6. I hate people who are always late.
7. Kevin has an uncle who used to be a boxing champion.
8. She found a letter in her letterbox which she read at once.

6 *Connect these sentences with the help of relative pronouns. (Sometimes there are several possibilities.)*

1. Cambridge University is world famous. It has many different colleges.
   Cambridge University, which is world famous, has many different colleges. / Cambridge University, which has many different colleges, is world famous.
2. Our town hall burnt down last week. It was built in the 14th century.
3. Our French teacher is married to a Frenchwoman. He spends most of his holidays in France.
4. This is her first poem. She wrote it when she was ten.
5. Mark is four years old. He can already write his name.
6. Bungee jumping is very dangerous. It is nevertheless very popular.

The relative pronouns *who, which* and *that* in defining relative clauses GG 131; GhE 309.1

7 *Put in a relative pronoun. (Sometimes there are several possibilities.)*

1. Many politicians criticize the awful conditions . . . exist in this country.
2. If they can't do it, they'll find someone . . . can.
3. The meeting was held in a conference room . . . was on the very top floor of the new office building.
4. Kate got married to a pilot . . . she had met at Heathrow airport.
5. The plane . . . has just landed has come from Dubai.
6. The police are looking for the person . . . damaged our neighbours' car.
7. The man . . . owns this villa is from South Africa.
8. Where are the sausages . . . I put in the fridge?
9. Sorry, I just can't remember the name of the lady . . . rang this morning.
10. They're looking for someone . . . they can really trust.

Contact clauses GG 132; GhE 309.2

8 *In which of these sentences can the relative pronoun be left out?*

1. People who live in glass houses shouldn't throw stones.
2. Earthwatch is an organization which supports research projects.
3. The humming birds which we saw at the zoo last week were as small as bumble bees.
4. The White Tower, which William the Conqueror built in the 11th century, is the oldest part of the Tower of London.
5. Rail strikes are especially annoying for people who travel to work by train every day.
6. Are these the glasses which you have been looking for?
7. The programmes that I like best are always on late at night.
8. Have you found the keys that you lost?

9 *Add a relative pronoun and commas where needed:*

1. The film . . . I watched last night wasn't really worth seeing.
2. The Clarendon Hotel . . . you can see at the top of the hill appeared in an Agatha Christie film.
3. My mother's doctor . . . I talked to on the phone last night said she was recovering from the operation very well.
4. Rugby is a game . . . doesn't interest me at all.
5. There's a bookshop round the corner . . . also sells videos.
6. The flowers . . . I gave my mother are still fresh.
7. I like the book . . . you lent me.
8. Mrs Baxter . . . lives next door has been taken to hospital.
9. Mr Hall is the neighbour . . . always complains about the noise . . . we make.

Prepositions in relative clauses
GG 133; GhE 311

10 *Give definitions of the following, using the words in brackets:*

1. chair (piece of furniture / sit on)
   A chair is a piece of furniture (that/which) you (can) sit on.
2. broom (brush / sweep the floor with)
3. dictionary (book / look up words in)
4. ambulance (vehicle / take patients to hospital in)
5. coffee table (table / serve coffee on)
6. shampoo (kind of soap / wash your hair with)
7. doormat (thing / wipe your feet on)
8. frying pan (pan / fry steaks in)
9. handkerchief (little cloth / blow your nose in)
10. brick (kind of stone / build houses with)

11 *These sentences do not sound very natural. Rephrase them by changing the position of the preposition. (In some cases you have to change – or leave out – the relative pronoun as well.)*

1. The video to which he referred is not in the library.
2. The concert to which I've been looking forward has unfortunately been cancelled.
3. The painting at which we looked last week was sold at the auction for £ 100,000.
4. The girl with whom Terry has fallen in love is a friend of my sister's.
5. The friends about whom I told you in my last letter will be visiting us next month.
6. The church at which you are looking now was built in Saxon times.
7. The financial difficulties into which the company had run were quite serious.

Relative clauses with *whose, of whom, of which*
GG 135; GhE 312

12 *Connect the sentences using relative clauses. (In some cases there are two possibilities.)*

1. This is Mr McLaverty. His house burnt down last night.
   This is Mr McLaverty, whose house burnt down last night.
2. The children started throwing snowballs. One of them hit and injured a little girl.
3. Antonio speaks Italian very well. His parents live in Rome.
4. We heard a lot of musicians at the rock festival. Some of them were really good.
5. Mrs Taylor has written two novels. Both of them are bestsellers.
6. The police found a car. Its windscreen was smashed.
7. We stopped to give a lift to an elderly couple. Their car had broken down.
8. Last week I met Tim Smith. I had gone to university with his brother.
9. She has a lot of friends on the town council. Many of them are quite influential.
10. The company is working on a new car. Its low cost will make it attractive to customers.

Defining relative clauses: revision
GG 131–133, 135; GhE 309, 311–312

13 *Rephrase the answers to these questions, using relative clauses with the noun phrases in brackets as antecedents:*

1. Who are the Kealeys? – We met them in Greece last year. (the people)
   They're the people (who/whom/that) we met in Greece last year.
2. What's the use of a modem? – It connects you to other computer users all over the world. (a device)

3. Mr Fletcher is a widower. – What's a widower? – His wife has died. (a man)
4. Is the parcel for you? – Yes, I've been waiting for it since Tuesday. (the parcel)
5. Do you know that man? – Yes, his photo is on the front page of all the newspapers today. (the man)
6. Who is Mrs Mallory? – Her husband is being searched for by the police. (the woman)
7. Do you like boxing? – No, I'm not interested in it at all. (a sport)
8. What do you think of my new assistant? – I think you can rely on her. (a person)
9. Is it true that your parents are thinking of getting divorced? – Yes, it worries me very much. (a problem)
10. Haven't we seen that girl before? – Yes, she served us at Woolworth's yesterday. (the shop assistant)

Relative clauses without an antecedent (relative clauses with *which* referring to a whole sentence, *whoever, whatever, whichever*)
GG 136–137; GhE 313–315

14 *Put in* which, whoever, whichever *or* whatever:

1. My mother accused me of having left the back door open, . . . simply wasn't true.
2. She always contradicts me, . . . I say.
3. . . . told you that is a liar.
4. Drink . . . you like.
5. We've got coke, orange juice, grape juice and apple juice. You can have . . . you like.
6. David Hill is going to go climbing in the Himalayas, . . . could be rather dangerous.
7. You can ask . . . you like – everyone will be against it.
8. He couldn't defend himself, . . . made him angry.
9. Take this plastic brush or . . . it is and throw it away, please.
10. . . . of the parts in the play you choose, it will mean learning a lot of lines.

15 *Translate these sentences into German:*

1. Unsere Nachbarn haben uns zum Brunch eingeladen, was wir sehr nett finden.
2. Was er auch sagen mag, glaube ihm nicht.
3. Du kannst zwischen drei Hauptgerichten *(main courses)* wählen. Nimm [dir], was du am liebsten magst.
4. Er beschwert sich ständig, was ich auch tue.
5. Henry kam sehr spät, was uns nicht überraschte.
6. Ich habe Nasi Goreng bestellt, was immer das sein mag.
7. Er versprach, sofort anzurufen, was er [auch] tat.

Chapter 16: Affirmative and negative statements, questions, shortened sentences

Affirmative and negative statements
GG 138 (83, 84, 89); GhE 19 (227, 229)

1 *Make negative statements using the sentences on the left and the crossed-out expressions on the right:*

1. Emma and Glen went to the theatre last night. *They didn't go to the cinema.*	~~cinema~~
2. Tom had cornflakes for breakfast.	~~egg~~
3. She can speak French and Italian.	~~Chinese~~
4. I have read "Romeo and Juliet".	~~"A Midsummer Night's Dream"~~
5. We know London very well.	~~Paris~~
6. He always has a shower after tennis.	~~bath~~
7. Joanne enjoys swimming very much.	~~cycling~~
8. I have been to England recently.	~~the USA~~
9. Sarah was waiting for John.	~~Carl~~
10. It looks like rain.	~~snow~~
11. Sandra will be moving next spring.	~~in the winter~~
12. She cut her hair herself yesterday.	~~have it cut~~
13. We must go to school every morning.	~~on Saturdays and Sundays~~
14. You may play in the garden now, Timmy.	~~in the street~~

Imperative sentences
GG 139; GhE 35

2 *Use affirmative or negative imperatives or* let's *in the following situations. These words will help you:*

> be (3×), cycle, feed, forget,
> have (2×), sit, touch,
> a drink, a piece, down, late, on,
> the animals, quiet, silly,
> the paintings, to do your homework

1. You're watching a good film on TV, but your little brother is making a lot of noise.
   You say: *Be quiet.*
2. An attendant in a museum sees some children moving very close to the paintings. He says: . . .
3. A sign in a zoo says: . . .
4. Your little sister wants to have some honey on her fish fingers. You say: . . .
5. You've been cycling for three hours with a friend. You see a nice pub and suggest: . . .
6. But it's getting dark and cold and your friend says: . . .
7. You have bought some chocolate and say to a friend: . . .
8. Your sister is going to a party. Your parents want her to be home by 11. They say: . . .
9. Your mother has just repainted a garden seat. You want to sit down, but she warns you: . . .
10. A teacher reminds her students: . . .

Yes/no questions

GG 140; GhE 21–22

3 *Join the questions to the appropriate answers:*

1. Is it snowing?
2. Must we do all the exercises?
3. Can the Millers speak French?
4. Should I try again?
5. Shall we go to the swimming-pool?
6. Does Joan often have headaches?
7. Did Derek make a lot of mistakes in the test?
8. Doesn't their cat eat mice?
9. Do you think Nicole would like this present?
10. Didn't Patrick remember to cut the grass yesterday?

a) Oh yes, let's.
b) No, they can't.
c) I don't know. Ask him yourself.
d) Yes, I'm sure she would.
e) No, you needn't.
f) Yes, you definitely should.
g) Oh, I think he forgot to.
h) Yes, I'm afraid she does.
i) No, she doesn't. She only eats hamburgers.
j) Yes. Look out of the window.

4 *What do you ask in these situations? Make up affirmative or negative* yes/no *questions.*

1. You wonder if you're late.
   Am I late?
2. You really think that Jane should have come by now.
   Shouldn't Jane have come by now?
3. You want to know if Mr Black works here.
4. You can't see Tony anywhere. Perhaps he's working in the garden.
5. You can't believe that Sarah has a bath twice a day.
6. You wonder whether the weather will be fine tomorrow.
7. You want to have the picnic here. You ask the others.
8. You can't believe that your brother can't do this simple exercise.
9. You are astonished that Mark doesn't like chocolate.
10. You wonder whether your father told your mother about the accident. (You ask him when you're alone with him.)
11. You find it difficult to believe that Clare didn't ring up last night.

Questions with question words

GG 141; GhE 24–25

5 *Ask questions about the underlined phrases:*

1. The Hendersons went to Australia last year.
   Where did the Hendersons go last year?
2. It took them 18 hours to get there.
3. The tickets cost them £ 1,500.
4. They had to leave at 2 o'clock in the morning.
5. They had to change planes in Singapore.
6. In Sydney they hired a Landrover.
7. They took a lot of water along because they knew that the outback can be very dangerous.
8. In the desert they met an aborigine.
9. The aborigine helped them to find the way to Ayers Rock.
10. Ayers Rock looked like a huge red balloon in the setting sun.
11. Mr Henderson had to stay in his hotel room for two days because he had a very bad sunstroke.
12. They want to go back to Australia next year.

6 *Fill in* what, which *or* who:

1. . . . would you like to eat?
2. . . . is that girl's name?
3. . . . way shall we go? Left or right?

4. . . . was that on the phone?
5. . . . colour is your new car?
6. . . . of you has got the keys to the gym?
7. . . . car does she drive?
8. . . . nationality is Benito?
9. . . . did you talk to after the concert?
10. . . . country did Captain Cook discover – Australia or India?
11. . . . do those fish fingers taste like?
12. . . . waiter served us, this one or that one over there?

Question tags GG 142; GhE 27–28

7 *Add question tags to the following sentences:*

1. The children are playing in the garden, *aren't they*?
2. You won't be late tonight, . . .
3. Mrs White works in Cambridge, . . .
4. She used to work in London before, . . .
5. Let's have something to drink, . . .
6. You didn't meet Pat at the party, . . .
7. So she won't be coming on the trip, . . .
8. They always have lunch at 1 o'clock, . . .
9. He never washes his car himself, . . .
10. There's a James Bond film on TV tonight, . . .
11. Come and see us at the weekend, . . .
12. He doesn't really say things like that, . . .
13. I am early, . . . (cf. GG 83A1; GhE 252)
14. You'd better go now, . . .

8 *Use the words in brackets to form sentences with question tags so that they fit the answers:*

1. (beautiful morning) – Yes, it's lovely. *It's a beautiful morning, isn't it?*
2. (Helen – not ring up) – No. Not while I was at home.
3. (Henry – live – Sydney) – No, he lives in Melbourne.
4. (your parents – on holiday) – Yes, they are in Florida.
5. (have – tea) – Oh yes, let's. Good idea.
6. (post office – near here) – Yes, just round the corner.
7. (be on time) – Don't worry. I'll be punctual.
8. (Mrs Barker – work – here) – Yes. Her office is on the third floor.
9. (Clare – play – piano – well) – Oh yes. She's fantastic.
10. (Sue – born – Detroit) – I don't think so. I think she was born in England.
11. (an older brother) – No, not as far as I know. He's an only child.
12. (go skiing – tomorrow) – Yes, I think we can. There'll be enough snow.

Short answers GG 143; GhE 29

9 *Give short answers to the following questions:*

1. Did you eat all the pudding? – Yes, . . .
2. Shouldn't he have rung up? – Yes, . . .
3. Will the weather be fine tomorrow? – No, . . .
4. Will you be all right with £ 50? – No, . . .
5. Is there a filling station near here? – No, . . .
6. Have you had a bath? – Yes, . . .
7. Was Cedric born in Ireland? – No, . . .
8. Has she got a car? – Yes, . . .
9. Can Joan ski well? – Yes, . . .
10. Would you tell her if you were me? – No, . . .
11. Was that supposed to be a joke? – No, . . .
12. Is he going to make lunch? – Yes, . . .
13. Are you ready to start now? – No, . . .
14. Must we learn all the irregular verbs? – No, . . .
15. Must Pete stay till the end of the performance? – No, . . .
16. May we go home now? – No, . . .

Short sentences with *so, nor, neither*
GG 144; GhE 34

10 *Add short sentences to the following statements, using* so, nor *or* neither *and the words in brackets:*

1. Gill loves music. (Pamela)
   So does Pamela.
2. Hank must go now. – (I)
3. I'm very thirsty. – (I)
4. Pat can do the job easily. – (Chris)
5. Dick helped me when I needed him. (Andy)
6. I've never had haggis. – (I)
7. Sue isn't coming to the party tomorrow. (Mike)
8. Wendy should really smoke less. – (you)
9. Our CD player needs repairing. – (our TV)
10. They never have meat on Friday. – (we)
11. Dick never got over the shock. (his girlfriend)
12. Tracy can't swim. – (her brother)
13. We don't like fast food much. – (we)
14. We didn't see the Queen when we visited Buckingham Palace. – (I)
15. I won't be at home tonight. – (my sister)
16. We were hoping to see the Changing of the Guard. – (we)
17. I thought the play was very exciting. – (I)

11 *Find the pairs of sentences that go together*

1. Jim didn't send us a Christmas card.	a) But Mark loves them.
2. Martina will be late tonight.	b) But her husband doesn't.
3. John sounds pretty disappointed.	c) So did Tim.
4. We aren't very keen on heavy metal.	d) We don't either.
5. San Diego is very hot in the summer.	e) I went there, too.
	f) So will Doris.
6. Mike gave her a nice Christmas present.	g) We aren't either.
7. When we were in San Francisco we went to Fisherman's Wharf.	h) Nor did Roberta.
8. They don't often bother with lunch on Sundays.	i) But Sue doesn't.
9. She loves lying on the beach doing nothing.	j) Santa Fé is too.
10. I don't like cheeseburgers.	

12 *Translate these sentences, using question tags or short answers where possible:*

1. Disney World ist in Orlando, oder?
2. Ich bin noch nie in Florida gewesen. – Ich auch nicht.
3. Kann man in der Sierra Nevada Bären sehen? – Ja.
4. Uns hat [der] Bryce Canyon besser gefallen als der Grand Canyon. – Uns auch.
5. Martina war ein Jahr als au pair in den USA. – Nicola auch.
6. Liegt (Ist) die Hauptstadt der USA im Staat Washington. – Nein.
7. In New York gibt es [doch] eine U-Bahn?
8. Der Kongress ist in Washington. – Der Oberste Gerichtshof auch.
9. Der Senat ist [ein] Teil des Kongresses, nicht wahr?
10. Der Präsident und seine Familie leben im Weißen Haus, oder nicht?

Chapter 17: From sentence to text (linking and emphasis)

Conjunctions and adverbs used to link sentences or parts of a sentence

GG 145; GhE 122A2, 151.2, 161–162, 329

1 *Put in a suitable conjunction or adverb, choosing from this list:*

after all, and, anyway, both . . . and, but, either . . . or, for, however, neither . . . nor, nevertheless, on the one hand . . . on the other hand, or, so, therefore, though, yet

In some cases there are several solutions.

1. Would you like to take your own car . . . would you prefer to rent a car?
2. I was very tired, . . . my back was aching.
3. They looked for a place to spend the night, . . . it was getting dark.
4. I'd like to go to the rock concert on Friday, . . . I'm afraid all the tickets have already been sold.
5. I don't think I'll manage to come on time – I'll try, ...
6. Taking a taxi won't make much difference because we'll be late . . . .
7. The manager said he would contact us, but he . . . telephoned . . . sent a fax.
8. He earns a lot of money, . . . he can afford expensive trips.
9. They had very little in common, but he loved her . . . .
10. Everything around him was blown to pieces; . . . the president escaped without a scratch.
11. We have a growing population, and . . . we need more food and water.
12. If you want to contact her, you can . . . ring her up at the office . . . meet her at the club.
13. After some arguments her parents finally agreed to Catherine leaving home. . . . she was no longer a child.
14. Living in a city has its advantages and disadvantages. . . . cities offer a lot of conveniences, but . . . they breed crime and violence.
15. He does his job very well. He works . . . fast . . . carefully.
16. So far she has been rather successful. . . ., she will have to work a lot harder to reach the top.

2 *Put in the correct equivalent of the German adverb* auch*:*

1. He is an English teacher, and his wife speaks English, ...
2. I like the red pullover, but the blue one is . . . very nice.
3. My mother grows flowers in her garden and all kinds of vegetables . . . .
4. He's hopeless at skiing, and he's not a good swimmer . . . .
5. I wasn't convinced that the plan would work. Henry, . . ., was sceptical.
6. She wrote him several letters and tried to phone him, ...
7. I can't stand cabbage. – I don't like it very much . . . .
8. The forget-me-not, . . . called scorpion grass, is a small plant with hairy leaves and tiny blue flowers.

The *there* construction

GG 146; GhE 341–342

3 *Translate these sentences, starting with a* there *construction:*

1. An der Bushaltestelle stand ein alter Mann.
   There was an old man standing at the bus stop.

2. Gibt es hier in der Nähe ein Postamt? – Ja, um die Ecke ist eines.
3. Es sind keine Sandwiches übrig.
4. Vor der Schule parkte ein großer grüner Lastwagen.
5. Es wohnen zur Zeit sehr wenige Gäste im Hotel.
6. Bei der Konferenz wurden einige gute Vorschläge gemacht.
7. Heute bläst ein kalter Wind.
8. Auf dem Tisch lagen ein paar Zeitungen.
9. Einige Kinder schwammen im See.
10. Morgen wird es eine große Überraschung geben.

The *it is/it was* construction

GG 147; GhE 339, 340.1

4 *Correct the following sentences, using the* it is/it was *construction and the words in brackets:*

1. Benjamin Franklin discovered the law of gravity in the 18th century. (Isaac Newton)
   It was Isaac Newton who discovered the law of gravity in the 18th century.
2. Dickens wrote "David Copperfield" between 1859 and 1860. (between 1849 and 1850)
3. In the 1970s the British discovered oil in the North Sea. (in the 1960s)
4. Thomas Edison invented the telephone in 1876 (Alexander Graham Bell)
5. Charles Lindbergh made the first powered flight in 1903. (the Wright Brothers)
6. Rock'n'roll became popular in the 1940s. (in the 1950s)
7. The Titanic sank after colliding with another ship. (after colliding with an iceberg)
8. The Danes invaded England in 1066. (the Normans)

Emphatic use of *do*

GG 148; GhE 335–336

5 *Emphasize one verb in each of these sentences or sequences of sentences by using a form of* do:

1. I bought a ticket, but I must have lost it.
   I did buy a ticket, but I must have lost it.
2. My grandfather owns, or rather owned, a Rolls Royce.
3. Why didn't you write to me? – Well, I wrote to you, but maybe the letter got lost in the post.
4. I knew that they were planning a new university library. But I hadn't realized that it would be built in the city centre.
5. I didn't think that my dad would repair my bike. But surprisingly enough, he repaired it.
6. We didn't like the band very much, but we liked the trumpet player.

Inversion as a stylistic device

GG 149; GhE 337.3, 338.3

6 *Put the negative or restricting adverbials into front position in order to make the sentences more emphatic.*

1. The match had hardly ended when it started to rain.
2. We had no sooner crossed the bridge than it collapsed.
3. One seldom sees daffodils in flower so early in the year.
4. They were speechless when they saw the temple. They had never seen anything so beautiful before.
5. She was full of hatred for that man. He had not only ruined her own life, but he had wrecked her daughter's, too.

Chapter 18: Reported speech

Statements in reported speech
GG 150–151; GhE 320, 322–324

1 *Put these sentences into reported speech, using the given introductory clauses:*

1. "I hate curry." – Sandra said . . .
2. Don't bring dogs into this restaurant. – The notice says . . .
3. "I feel sick." – Kevin said . . .
4. "I'm going to California for three months." – Wendy has told me . . .
5. "Sorry, I won't be able to play on Saturday. I've had an accident." – Tony has told me . . .
6. "I'm really good at playing the guitar." – He keeps telling people . . .
7. "I would like to talk to the manager, please." – The lady said . . .
8. "You've done the essay awfully well." – Tomorrow her teacher will say . . .
9. "You are simply lazy." – Our maths teacher kept complaining . . .
10. "I'll be back by nine, love Brian." – The note said . . .
11. "I would like to come and see you all on Sunday." – Aunt Margaret had told us . . .
12. "I'm going to bring my dogs along." – She had warned us . . .
13. Hurricanes expected in Florida tomorrow. – The headline says . . .
14. Do not overheat pan. – The instructions say . . .
15. "I'm so terribly fond of all my pets, you know." – She kept telling us . . .
16. Our diet tends to be unbalanced, and we eat far too much sugar. – The article explains . . .
17. No parking in this area. – The notice over there says . . .
18. "You are stupid, Timmy." – "Mummy, Nick always says . . ."

2 *Fill in the correct form of* say *or* tell*:*

1. She . . . Jack that she was going away for a few days.
2. They . . . they would be home for supper.
3. Amy . . . she would have to be back in London next month.
4. The notice . . . that we mustn't leave the car here after dark.
5. Uncle Dave . . . us he had once seen the Beatles live in the 60s.
6. I . . . Mum that I would go to the cinema with Ann.
7. The weather forecast . . . that tomorrow will be warm and sunny.
8. Tracy rang up at 7. She . . . she was too tired to come round tonight.
9. The instructions . . . we must first plug in and **then** switch on.
10. George is on the phone. He . . . he has got to the station on an earlier train. But he . . . that he doesn't need collecting.
11. The girl at the reception desk . . . that Mr Singh wasn't in.
12. The secretary . . . that the guests had arrived and were waiting in the hall.
13. We keep . . . them that they mustn't park their car in our drive.
14. The police . . . the press that they were asking the public for help with this case.

3 *First read the following text:*

Glenda Lawson interviews Randy Cokes, the enfant terrible of English football.

Glenda: Is it true, Randy, that your relationship to the press is – well – a little troubled?

Randy: The press has written a lot of rubbish about me recently. And I'm not going to talk to the press in the future.

Glenda: Well, thank you for making an exception – and giving me this exclusive interview. How do you feel, Randy?

Randy: I feel great. OK, I may be a little overweight at the moment. But that is no problem at all.

Glenda: Well, isn't it true that you were dropped from the team because you had put on an extra 12 kilos or so?

Randy: That's one of those absurd exaggerations. I wasn't in shape because of my knee injury in the winter.

Glenda: What about the rumours about you seeing rather a lot of Miranda, the Spanish model, and your marriage breaking up?

Randy: That's all a lot of nonsense. I love my wife – and there is no question of divorce. Miranda is a good friend of the family. She actually went to school with my wife.

Glenda: Did she? I didn't know that. But tell me about what happened in that bar in Manchester. You know, after you lost against United.

Randy: Well, there the press goes again. There was nothing in it. I just had a little argument with this United fan –

Glenda: – who apparently had a broken nose and a few teeth missing.

Randy: That's all been settled. Everybody needs a bit of fun sometimes.

Glenda: Then there was that speeding incident. You were doing 140 mph on the M1.

Randy: Actually, it was only 130. And, O.K., it was my car. But I wasn't driving. It was Miranda.

Glenda: Tell me about your contacts abroad. There was some talk about you wanting to play in Spain.

Randy: There's nothing in it. It's true I was rung up by some people from Barcelona, but I love playing in Britain – and what they offered me was simply ridiculous.

Glenda: Well, thank you, Randy, and good luck.

Now complete this summary of what Randy told Glenda:

1. Randy said that the press . . . and that . . . .
2. Talking about his health, he said . . . . He admitted . . ., but . . . .
3. Randy complained that the talk of him being so overweight . . . and that . . . .
4. He explained that the rumours about him and Miranda . . . . He said . . . and that. . . . He explained that Miranda . . . . and . . . .
5. When asked about the famous bar incident, Randy explained . . ., that he . . . and that now everything . . . . He said that . . . .
6. About the speeding incident, he said that . . . and that . . ., but that he . . . . It . . . .
7. When questioned about the talks with Barcelona, Randy said . . . although . . . . He explained . . . and that . . . .

4 *Use reported speech to express surprise or disappointment in the following situations. Use these expressions:*

be in Wales, be in love with Steve, be on a diet, be ready today, hate fish, not like the heat, not want to see each other ever again, stop smoking

1. "We're going to Spain in the summer holidays." – "Really, but I thought your parents *didn't like the heat.*"
2. "I'm sorry, but we haven't been able to look at your car yet." – "But when I brought it in yesterday you said . . ."
3. "Can you give me a cigarette?" – "What? I thought . . ."
4. "Jack and Sue are getting married this Saturday." – "Didn't you tell me not long ago . . ."
5. "There's a new fish restaurant in the High Street. Shall we go there for lunch on Sunday?" – "I always thought . . ."
6. "You know, Martin is living in England. He's doing a year at Cardiff University." – "Did you say Cardiff? I thought . . ."
7. "I'm terribly hungry. Let's get something nice to eat." – "Are you serious? This morning you told me . . ."
8. "I'm going out with Dan tonight, Mum." – "How strange, yesterday you said . . ."

5 *Report what Tom, a boy you met at the youth club last night, told you about himself. In many cases there are two possibilities. (Ask yourself if backshift is necessary or possible at all.)*

1. "I love playing basketball." – Tom told me . . .
2. "I play for our school team." – He said . . .
3. "But I haven't got much time to practise. So I'm no longer playing for the county." – He also said . . .
4. "You know, my marks at school were getting worse with all the sport I was doing." – He went on to say . . .
5. "So I really should work harder if I want to get decent A-level results." – He realizes . . .
6. "Last year I was in the drama group. I enjoyed that a lot." – He told me . . .
7. "I'm hoping to go to America for a year." – He said . . .
8. "Perhaps I'll be able to get a scholarship at an American university." – He thought . . .
9. "Maybe I can play basketball in America." – He hopes . . .
10. "I may even stay in the States for more than a year." – He added . . .
11. "I really would have liked to be a professional basketball player." – He said . . .
12. "But I'm afraid I'm not good enough." – But he's afraid . . .

6 After the Italian cruise ship "Mona Lisa" had sunk in the Indian Ocean, there were complaints and accusations about the fitness of the ship and the behaviour of the crew.

a) *Change the report back into direct speech.*
b) *Translate sentences 1–4 into German.*

1. Some English holiday-makers said that there had been no food and no water in the lifeboats.
   "There was no food and no water in the lifeboats."
2. They added that some of the lifeboats had been old and rusty.
3. An old American lady complained that she had been pushed aside by crew members who had wanted to get into a lifeboat before her.
4. Some German passengers, on the other hand, praised the crew and one of them said that he had seen the captain coming out of the engine room with a black face. And that the captain had been the last to leave the ship.
5. An American couple said they had been saving up for the cruise for years. But that they would never in their lives go on board a ship again.
6. Tony Nobles, the Daily Star reporter, who happened to be on board, said that he had heard children cry and that passengers had been running from one side of the ship to the other in panic. He thought that the crew had been absolutely useless.
7. Captain Giovanni Forza, when questioned in Mombasa yesterday, said that there was no foundation whatsoever to the criticism.
8. He admitted, however, that he had been late sending out the SOS, because he had thought the crew would get the fire under control.
9. He added that it had been very difficult for his crew to put the fire out because a lot of the fire fighting equipment had been destroyed by the fire.
10. He explained that members of the crew and passengers had tried to put the fire out with buckets of water. And that he had given that order to keep the passengers occupied and so to prevent panic.
11. But a group of Dutch passengers said that they were unconvinced and that they would go to court and claim damages. *(Schadensansprüche stellen).*
12. Italy's minister for transport, Guiseppe Vaporetto, announced that he himself would head a government commission to investigate the circumstances of the loss of the "Mona Lisa".

Questions and commands in reported speech GG 152; GhE 327

7 *Use reported speech to express what Ray tells Alice about his mother's questions. Use introductory clauses with* asked me, wondered *or* wanted to know. *Decide whether to use backshift or not.*

1. Are you going to see Alice this weekend?
   My mother wanted to know whether I was going to see you this weekend.
2. Will she be at Mark's party?
   She wondered whether you would be at Mark's party.
3. When did you last see her?
4. Does she still live in that tiny bedsitter in Hammersmith?
5. How long have you known her now?
6. How are her parents?
7. What do they do for a living? And what do you think of them?
8. Did you really enjoy your trip to Rome with Alice?
9. Is she still working at that funny place in Soho?
10. How old is she now?
11. You aren't going to marry her, are you?
12. Where did you first meet her?
13. Shall I give her a message if she should ring up?

8 *Report these questions, using the given introductory clauses and infinitive constructions:*

1. "How shall I do exercise 3?"
   He asked the teacher *how to do exercise 3.*
2. "Which colour should I choose?"
   She didn't know ...
3. "Where shall we put our bikes?"
   The boys were unsure ...
4. "Could you please help me in the garden?"
   My father asked me ...
5. "Can you lend me your car on Saturday?"
   Helen asked her boyfriend ...
6. "Shall we do the job now or later?"
   The workmen asked the boss ...
7. "Shall we give her some chocolates or some flowers?"
   They wondered ...
8. "Where can I ask for advice?"
   The lady didn't know ...
9. "Should I buy the green vase or the blue one?"
   The customer could not make up her mind ...
10. "Can you tell me how I can get back onto the motorway?"
    The driver asked the policeman ...

9 *Put these commands into reported speech. Use the past tense of the verbs in brackets in the introductory clause.*

1. Girl to boyfriend: "Please don't be late again." (ask)
   The girl asked her boyfriend not to be late again.
2. Driving instructor to pupil: "Don't drive too slowly in the test." (warn)
3. Wife to husband: "Please take the dog to the vet's on Thursday." (remind)
4. Teacher to pupils: "Look at all the irregular verbs again before the test." (advise)
5. Boss to secretary: "Please post all those letters straight away." (ask)
6. Traffic warden to driver: "Don't leave your car in the drive, madam." (tell)
7. Dog owner to pet: "Sit, Bonzo!" (order)
8. Landlady to guest: "Have a cup of coffee, dear." (ask)
9. Flight attendant to forgetful passenger: "Fasten your seatbelt please, sir." (remind)
10. Mother to son: "Please don't put your elbows on the table." (ask)

The shift of expressions of time and place in reported speech

GG 153; GhE 325–326

10 Nancy and Simon have been married for some time now. But they often think and talk about the first little argument that they had in their student days.

Put what they said into reported speech:

1. Simon: "Can we go to the cinema tonight, Nancy?"
   I asked you whether we could go to the cinema that night.
2. Nancy: "I'm sorry, but I've got choir practice today."
   And I answered that I was sorry, but that I had choir practice that day.
3. Simon: "What about tomorrow? Have you got time tomorrow?"
4. Nancy: "Well, actually, I've arranged to see Mike tomorrow evening."
5. Simon: "But I haven't seen you at all this week! What have you been doing all the time?"
6. Nancy: "Please keep your voice down. I'm not your property, you know. And I don't feel like arguing with you here in the library."
7. Simon: "OK, OK. But what did you do yesterday"?
8. Nancy: "You know I've had flu all this week, and I only got up for the first time yesterday."
9. Simon: "But the last time we went out together must have been last month."
10. Nancy: "It was on Saturday – ten days ago to be exact. And I told you that I don't want an argument in this place. So let's say no more about it. Shall we go and have lunch together?"

11 *Translate this newspaper article into English:*

Am 6. Dezember vergangenen Jahres wurde auf dem Weihnachtsmarkt[1] ein Mann bestohlen[2], beschimpft[3] und tätlich angegriffen[4]. Gestern fand die Gerichtsverhandlung[5] statt.

Der Kläger[6], Klaus Barber, etwa fünfzig Jahre alt, erklärte, er werde schon seit längerer Zeit von seinen Freunden „Nikolaus[7]" genannt, weil er einen so langen Bart[8] habe. Auch mache er Kindern gern eine Freude[9] und habe sich deshalb als Nikolaus verkleidet[10].

Er habe einen großen Sack voller Süßigkeiten [mit sich] getragen, die er tags zuvor für etwa 300,– DM gekauft habe.

Er sei sich sicher gewesen, dass die Kinder auf dem Weihnachtsmarkt sich über die Süßigkeiten freuen würden. Aber von nun an werde er sich diese Mühe nicht mehr machen[11].

Plötzlich seien die drei Angeklagten[12], drei 16-jährige Jungen, von hinten auf ihn losgestürzt[13], hätten ihn zu Boden geworfen und ihm den Sack entrissen[14]. Außerdem hätten sie ihn beschimpft und gerufen, er sei ein Penner[15].

Die Angeklagten beteuerten[16], sie seien unschuldig[17]. Der Mann mit dem Bart habe ihnen den Sack geschenkt, weil sie so freundlich zu ihm gewesen seien.

Eine Zeugin[18] sagte aus[19], sie sei eine alte Frau und könne nicht mehr so gut sehen, aber sie habe die drei Jungen erkannt. Sie hätten mit dem Sack auf einer Bank im Park gesessen und sich über den Nikolaus lustig gemacht[20].

Der Richter[21] fragte die Jungen, ob sie bei ihrer Aussage bleiben[22] wollten. Als sie dies verneinten, verurteilte er sie wegen tätlicher Beleidigung[23]. Er forderte sie auf[24], an den vier Wochenenden vor Weihnachten in einem Altersheim[25] zu arbeiten und ermahnte[26] sie, nie wieder so etwas zu tun.

[1] Christmas fair; [2] rob; [3] abuse; [4] assault; [5] trial; [6] plaintiff; [7] Father Christmas; [8] beard; [9] make s.o. happy; [10] dress up as; [11] not bother; [12] defendant; [13] pounce on s.o.; [14] snatch (away from); [15] bum; [16] assert; [17] not guilty; [18] witness; [19] state; [20] make fun of; [21] judge; [22] keep to a statement; [23] convict s.o. of assault; [24] tell; [25] old people's home; [26] warn

Appendix: False friends, traps and trouble spots

adverbs

Tom worked very **hard** before his exam.	**Tom** arbeitete vor seinem Examen sehr **schwer/hart**.
He had **hardly** any time for anything else.	Er hatte **kaum** Zeit für etwas anderes.
The shop assistant was very friendly.	Die Verkäuferin war sehr freundlich.
She served us **in a friendly way**.	Sie bediente uns **freundlich**.
Clare speaks French rather **badly**, but Ralph speaks it even **worse** than she does, and Tim speaks it **worst** of all.	Clare spricht ziemlich **schlecht** Französisch, aber Ralph spricht es noch **schlechter** als sie, und Tim spricht es **am schlechtesten** von allen.
Monica says very **little** in class, Jane says even **less**, and Chris says **least**.	Monica sagt im Unterricht sehr **wenig**, Jane sagt noch **weniger**, und Chris sagt **am wenigsten**.

articles

School starts at nine o'clock.	**Die Schule/Der Unterricht** beginnt um neun Uhr.
Her mother is **a teacher**.	Ihre Mutter ist **Lehrerin**.
History is full of violence and wars.	**Die Geschichte** ist voller Gewalt und Kriege.
Most people believe that **the most important** thing **in life** is to make a lot of money.	**Die meisten Menschen** glauben, **das Wichtigste im Leben** sei, viel Geld zu verdienen.

during – while

The Millers lived in the USA **during** the war.	Millers lebten **während** des Krieges in den USA.
While Sandra was working in the garden, she couldn't hear the telephone.	**Während** Sandra im Garten arbeitete, konnte sie das Telefon nicht hören.

each other – themselves

Judy and Patrick have known **each other** for years.	Judy und Patrick kennen **sich** seit Jahren.
They were amused when they saw **themselves** on TV.	Sie waren belustigt, als sie **sich** im Fernsehen sahen.

for – since

We have had our car **for seven years** now.	Wir haben unseren Wagen jetzt schon **seit** sieben Jahren/sieben Jahre lang.
They have been playing **since two o'clock**.	Sie spielen **seit** zwei Uhr.

German: Perfekt – English: Past Tense

I **saw** him in town yesterday.	Ich **habe** ihn gestern in der Stadt **gesehen**.
Did you **do** your homework last night?	**Hast** du gestern Abend deine Hausaufgaben **gemacht**?
We **went** to the seaside at the weekend.	Wir **sind** am Wochenende ans Meer **gefahren**.

German: Präsens – English: future forms

I think Liverpool **will win** the Cup Final.	Ich glaube, dass Liverpool den Cup Final **gewinnt**.
I'm going to buy myself a new bike this spring.	Ich **kaufe** mir dieses Frühjahr ein neues Fahrrad.
I'm playing tennis with Greg this afternoon.	Ich **spiele** heute Nachmittag mit Greg Tennis.
Next month **I'll be lying** on the beach in the South of France.	Nächsten Monat **liege** ich in Südfrankreich am Strand.

German: Präsens – English: Present Perfect

How long **have** you **known** him?	Wie lange **kennst** du ihn schon?
We **have lived/have been living** in Nottingham for two years/since 1994.	Wir **wohnen** seit zwei Jahren/seit 1994 in Nottingham.

German: *wollen, daß* – English: *want s.o. to do s.th.*

Her parents **want** Helen **to go** to university.	Ihre Eltern **wollen, dass** Helen **studiert**.
The traffic warden **doesn't want us to park** our car here.	Die Politesse **möchte nicht, dass wir** hier **parken**.

gerunds

My mother **suggested going** for a walk after lunch.	Meine Mutter **schlug vor,** nach dem Mittagessen spazieren **zu gehen**.
He was so nervous that he **avoided looking** at her.	Er war so nervös, dass er es **vermied**, sie **anzusehen**.
Thomas is frightfully **good at playing** the guitar.	Thomas **kann** unheimlich **gut** Gitarre **spielen**.
The film is really **worth seeing**.	**Es lohnt sich** wirklich, den Film **anzusehen**.
He was **looking forward to seeing** her again after his holidays.	Er **freute sich darauf,** sie nach den Ferien **wiederzusehen**.
I can't get **used to getting** up at 6 every morning.	Ich kann mich nicht daran **gewöhnen**, jeden Morgen um 6 **aufzustehen**.

let – make – have for German *lassen*

At the weekend my parents **let** me **sleep** as long as I like.	Am Wochenende **lassen** mich meine Eltern **schlafen**, solange ich will.